soapstars

soapstars

the making of an emmerdale star

lance parkin

BⵝXTREE

First published 2001 by Boxtree
an imprint of Pan Macmillan Ltd
20 New Wharf Road London N1 9RR
Basingstoke and Oxford

Associated companies throughout the world

In association with Granada Media Commercial Ventures

www.panmacmillan.com

ISBN 0 7522 6190 8

Soapstars is an LWT production in
association with Yorkshire Television.

Soapstars programme material
copyright © Granada Media Group Ltd

Text copyright © Pan Macmillan Ltd

9 8 7 6 5 4 3 2 1

A CIP catalogue record for this book
is available from the British Library.

Typeset by seagulls
Printed by Mackays of Chatham plc

contents

acknowledgements

The author would like to thank everyone at *Soapstars*, especially the producer, Tim Miller.

And to everyone at *Emmerdale*, particularly those who generously gave their time to help with this book: Samantha Giles, Patrick Mower, Keith Richardson, Steve Frost, Tim Fee, Chris Thompson, Lance Milligan, Tim Worsnop, Giles Latham, Karen Grimes, Wendy Bloom, Estelle Hind and Sarah Wooton.

Thanks to my editor, Katy Carrington, as well as Susanna Wadeson, Gordon Wise, Roseanne Boyle, Paula Gillespie and Jonathan Baker.

Thanks are also due to Vijay Amarnani, Hayley Chapman, Shane Chapman, Kelly Cox, Malcolm Dorkin, Joanne Farrelly, Ivan Garel-Jones, Nigel Jones, Christine Mathisen and Madeleine Pallas.

And for their photographs: Mike Alsford, Brian Geeves, Neil Genower, Ken McKay, Denzil McNeelance, Helen Turton and Mike Vaughan.

And Denise O'Donoghue at the *Big Breakfast*.

And, of course, thanks to the *Soapstars* themselves. It feels mean to single people out – but special thanks to Jon Miller, Maria Sophia Andreas, Andy White, Victoria Tonge, Vicki Greenwood, Emma Pollard, Ashra Price, Debra Michaels, Johnny Kinch, Brian McDevitt, Becky Weeks, Erin Lordan, Craig Henderson and Jo-Ann D'Costa. As well, of course, to the new family … (if you don't want to know the result, look away now) Dee Whitehead, Mark Jardine, Jason Hain, Ruth Abram and Elspeth Brodie.

'In the future everybody will be world famous for fifteen minutes.'

Andy Warhol, 1968

introduction

Friday 27 July 2001

The tabloid papers aren't sure what the big story of the day is – tonight is the grand finale of *Big Brother 2*, and the *Mirror* and the *Sun* are backing rival candidates Brian and Helen, listing their respective vices and virtues with a great deal more fervour than they used when covering the battle between Blair and Hague the previous month. In the event, around 8 million votes will be cast – an extraordinary turnout. But yesterday, another big story broke: Martin Kemp, the actor who plays Steve in *EastEnders*, announced that he's leaving the BBC soap and has signed an exclusive contract for ITV that will see him earning millions playing high-profile parts. It's a coup for the ITV network chiefs – but it's also good publicity for *EastEnders*, the week before the show starts broadcasting a fourth weekly episode. And if Martin Kemp is a draw for ITV viewers, then almost by definition, he's a draw for tabloid readers. Unable to decide which of these two events is the most momentous, the *Sun* splits its front page evenly between them.

Soap, reality TV and stars being lined up for an autumn ratings battle. There could scarcely be a more auspicious day for the last of the *Soapstars* open auditions. This has been a year in which soap opera and reality television have come to dominate the television schedules – *Soapstars* brings the two formats together.

Less than two months ago, the following advert appeared in the national press:

WANTED : SOAPSTARS

LWT are looking to cast a new family for one of ITV's top soaps. If you're aged 16 or over you could become a TV star. The nationwide search for a new talent starts next month. Auditions will be filmed for a primetime ITV series. For details call ...

The programme will be made by the TV company that produced last year's *Popstars*, and the prize is the same – a real chance for stardom, doing the sort of job that people dream of, and spend years working towards. What's on offer isn't a cameo appearance, or a couple of episodes. It's a proper contract for the Yorkshire Television soap *Emmerdale*, with the prospect of years in the series – if the actors are up to the job and their characters prove popular. It's not a gimmick, it's not a trick – it's the chance of a lifetime.

And people have responded. Around 6,000 have turned up at the open auditions. The crowds have stopped traffic; people have camped overnight, jumped the queues or scaled roofs to be here. Some people have trekked to more than one of the auditions, eager for a chance for fame and fortune. There are all sorts of people here, for all sorts of reasons: teenagers who want to be on TV; entertainers out to make a spectacle of themselves; people who've skipped school or work on the off-chance they'll make it; professional actors who've been trying for twenty years to get their big break; and those who are simply deluded.... 6,000 stories, 6,000 unique experiences, all competing for just five parts.

Getting the big break is a matter of being in the right place at the right time – and this will be it for the best five people. But is this an audition or a piece of entertainment? The producer of *Soapstars*, Tim Miller, argues that it's both. 'Throughout the whole process, we were being pulled in two completely different directions,' he explains. 'On the one hand, we needed to make interesting and entertaining television. On the other hand, we needed to devise an audition process that would enable our panel to make informed judgements about the actors. What made interesting TV wasn't always instructive for the judges. And what the judges wanted wouldn't always make for interesting TV.'

By now, the press have revealed that the leading soap in question is *Emmerdale*. Steve Frost, the producer of *Emmerdale*, is keen to be involved, but acknowledges that it won't be a straightforward process: 'It's an ambitious but exciting project and will possibly discover some genuinely talented people – though it's going to be complex to marry the production schedules and requirements of the two programmes. Hopefully we'll have some talented new actors and an exciting new family on screen, plus, of course, raised awareness of the programme.' However, Steve acknowledges that the series has had a stormy ride so at first: 'Not everybody thought it was a great idea and there was some negotiating to do to make sure that everybody was happy with the project.'

The process took four months, and saw the thousands of hopefuls whittled down to five actors, who have already taken their place in the cast of *Emmerdale*. The *Soapstars* television series charted the ups and downs, followed the winners and losers. But there's plenty we didn't get to see on television....

destination: emmerdale

CHAPTER ONE

Early 2001. The makers of Emmerdale *and the makers of* Soapstars *plan for the new family.*

Emmerdale is a place of work. One of the most efficient in the business. If the director of a Hollywood film manages to get three minutes of material in a day, he'll often be happy. Even for the average television drama, it's only possible to film five to eight minutes' worth of material every day. *Emmerdale* goes out five nights a week – and that means that twenty-four minutes has to be made every single working day. Not just recorded, but ideas have to be turned into scripts, the scripts are edited, then the production team work out the logistics of bringing the script to life, actors are given the scripts, and have to learn their lines and think how best to interpret them. Sets have to be dressed, engineers have to ensure the lighting and sound are perfect, cameramen have to do their job. Actors are given costumes and make-up, then the episodes have to be recorded, edited, viewed, made ready for broadcast.

Emmerdale is 'production-line television'. The term is often used somewhat sniffily, but *Emmerdale* is one of the top three programmes on TV. Ten million people watch it every night, and at seven every weekday evening, *Emmerdale* is the first shot in ITV's campaign for ratings. The *Emmerdale* people are proud of that. What's more, despite a relatively small per-episode budget, it's got the reputation of being the most visually lavish soap. It's no coincidence that if you walk into the lobby of the *Emmerdale* building, one of the first things you'll see is the BAFTA award they won earlier this year.

Making a television programme is quite an undertaking, and there are hundreds of people working on *Emmerdale*, including about fifty regular cast members. And if only one or two of those people aren't up to their job, it becomes immediately obvious to millions of people – if the cameraman can't focus, a sound man's always putting his boom in shot, an actor can't act or a writer can't write, then everyone else's efforts will be wasted.

Whoever gets the parts in *Soapstars* will be pitched into this environment, and they won't get any favours because of the unusual casting method. Just the opposite – the viewers will be scrutinizing them closely, knowing how and why they were cast, comparing them with the established actors, maybe even comparing them with other finalists who didn't make it through. There will be a special programme on the same night they are introduced; there will be particular interest from the press. Time after time in the following weeks, the hopefuls will be told that it's hard work and that they'll have to be up to the job.

Emmerdale's executive producer, Keith Richardson, the Group Controller of Drama, Yorkshire Tyne Tees Television. He worked as unit manager on the very first episode of the series, and has been executive producer since 1986. Keith isn't involved in the day-to-day running of the show. It's his job to oversee *Emmerdale*, to bring his experience to bear to keep the show on course. He appoints the producer, he attends long-term conferences, double-checks important casting decisions. He also fights the show's corner within YTV and at the ITV network. When major decisions are made, such as going to three and then five nights a week, or involving *Emmerdale* with *Soapstars*, it will be Keith Richardson who oversees the discussions on *Emmerdale*'s behalf, and who reaches the ultimate decision.

Keith is very pleased to be involved with *Soapstars*: 'We first heard about *Soapstars* soon after *Popstars* was a success,' he explains, 'and although we tried to keep to keep an air of mystery about it, the family was always going to end up in *Emmerdale*.

'I thought it was rather flattering to be asked – it demonstrates that we're a more flexible show than our rivals. That said, it's also a writer-driven show, so we talked to the writers about how we could go about introducing a family all in one go, bearing in mind the casting process and past experience. On the whole, the writers were enthusiastic, and we got a really useful list of benefits from those discussions.

'The main benefit to me was that it was an opportunity to reintroduce the holiday village, which I'd always thought was an entertaining setting for stories, and something unique to *Emmerdale*, but something we've not seen for a few years.

'My main concern was that the integrity of *Emmerdale* was maintained. *Soapstars* is going to be an entertaining programme. We've not got, and didn't want, editorial control over the *Soapstars* programmes, but we wanted to be certain that we're left with actors we can use on *Emmerdale*.

'There was also the worry that following on from *Popstars* this would be *Rocky 2* – that we wouldn't have the excitement and interest of the original, it would seem like second best.

'The ratings really weren't a consideration. Sure, it will raise *Emmerdale*'s profile, and get people who wouldn't normally talk about it to talk about it. We'll be in people's faces for a few weeks. For me, this is an honest try to get people interested in *Emmerdale*. It gives the people that are already watching a new family to watch and enjoy, keeps it fresh. A new audience might be exposed to *Emmerdale*, give us a try, and like what they see. But I'm not expecting a specific boost just from *Soapstars*.'

emmerdale's new family takes shape

When I started work on *Soapstars*,' producer Tim Miller explains, '*Emmerdale* had already expressed an interest. Initial talks had already taken place with executive producers at LWT. But *Emmerdale* said they would need to talk to the writers about it. We went up to film at a writers' meeting up in Leeds, and together with Keith and Steve we had to try to convince them that *Soapstars* might be good for *Emmerdale*.' As he recalls, there was strong initial opposition from some quarters to the whole idea of a marriage between *Soapstars* and an established soap such as *Emmerdale*. 'There were about thirty people at the meeting and the atmosphere was very hostile. We were bombarded with questions and it was all very frightening. Some people were clearly never going to be convinced, while others were fairly enthusiastic about the project.

One of their concerns was that we would be exposing the real people behind the soap characters and this might undermine the drama. But these days, soap actors are constantly in the papers and get enormous exposure in various magazines. This has only heightened the interest in soaps, not eroded it.

'From the outset, Keith said he wanted some input into the selection of the panel. It was important that someone from *Emmerdale* was involved – preferably one of the writers.'

In the end, *Emmerdale* ensured they had control over the process. Steve Frost: 'We had final approval of the panel's choice. As it happened there was a unanimous decision on the final five.'

Once the decision had been made, it was up to the makers of *Emmerdale* to make the new family work. Before you can cast actors you have to come up with the characters they'll be playing. This, of course, happens all the time in soaps. Steve explains: 'New characters are often introduced as part of stories for existing characters, or they can come in to bring something entirely new to the character mix. Once we decide that we want a new character, we refine exactly what that will be, what their role will be in the programme and what their story will be. In normal circumstances, once we have a character brief on paper and a story, we start the casting search and will see as many people as necessary through a series of meetings, auditions and camera tests until we decide on the right person for the role.'

Was Steve worried that people would watch *Emmerdale* thinking 'those are the people that won *Soapstars*'? 'Not at all. Nobody really watches thinking, "That's Liz Estensen from *The Liver Birds*" or "That's Peter Martin from *The Royle*

Family." TV audiences take for granted that they are watching people they know from other roles playing parts. Indeed, they love to do it – hence David Jason, John Thaw et al, all of whom are known as other characters than they are currently playing.'

One of the regular writers for *Emmerdale*, Chris Thompson, came up with the outline of the characters that made up the new family.

'The brief from Network was pretty inflexible,' Chris recalls. 'They wanted a family of five to six people and they had to be introduced at the same time.

'I thought of the adults first and I had the idea that they would be two thirty-five to forty-five-year-olds who were married to other people and finally made the break and went off to start a new life together. So their first day in the show is their first day as a couple.... Maggie has two children and Phil has one. The kids came later – much later – as we felt we had to establish the adults clearly first. But we thought there was loads of dramatic mileage in the situation of kids being thrown together, as in all new step-families.

'We needed somewhere for them to work and live and interact. We were conscious of the need for a new set for our growing number of young characters and decided to reintroduce the holiday village. Our characters arrive to work there and it meant we could play stuff in advance about the village being bought and re-opened in ways that involve our regular characters so that our new characters didn't walk into a void. There is a danger they'll be out on a limb but that danger exists in all new characters. We have done our best to mesh them into established characters/plots.

'The method of casting had no impact on the creation of the characters. They were created as they would have been for characters who would be cast in the conventional way. Not to have done that would have diminished the newcomers and the show.'

The last time *Emmerdale* introduced a family of a similar size was in 1999, with the introduction of the Reynoldses. As anyone who watches a soap knows, bringing in a whole new family, ready-made and all at once, can often cause problems – *Brookside* and *EastEnders* have, in the past, introduced a new family with much fanfare... only to see them all written out a few months later, or straining credibility by having the characters who aren't working leave, but keeping the rest. So, parents end up abandoning kids or perfectly healthy marriages split up. The problem is compounded by the fact that the storylines and scripts for *Emmerdale* have to be prepared months in advance. By the time a new character appears on screen, and the viewers have decided whether they like them or not, the storylines for the next fifty or sixty episodes will have been prepared – it's too late to pull the plug if it's a disaster. Even by the time a regular actor is cast, several dozen episodes will have been written for them.

Aware of this problem, the *Emmerdale* writers phased in the Reynolds family. First we saw Sean, the father of the family. He mentioned his wife and kids, though initially we never saw them. Sean was a haulier, a new rival for series villain Chris Tate. He was always intended as a regular character, and as soon as Stephen McGann was cast in the role, it was clear he would become an important part of the show. As Sean started to sabotage Tate Haulage, one particular policewoman was seen investigating the crimes... and

Chris was horrified to learn that she was Sean's wife, Angie – ably played by Freya Copeland.

Thereafter, we started to see Sean and Angie as a couple. By now, their kids had names – Marc and Ollie – but the characters themselves still weren't seen on screen. Within a few weeks, Anthony Lewis and Vicky Binns were cast, and we finally saw the whole Reynolds family together in their Hotten home. And a few weeks after that, when the producer and writers were happy the characters and actors were all working out, Sean bought a family home in Emmerdale itself.

Chris Thompson recalls the way the Reynolds family came into the series: 'I remember the Reynolds' introduction fondly and it was obviously easier to bring them in gradually; but [in the case of the *Soapstars* winners] that simply wasn't an option, although some writers felt strongly we should phase them in.

He goes on to describe how the new family took shape. 'The names were originally Dave and Maggie and they came out of my head – just like that – based on no one at all. (I almost never give names based on real people.) Dave became Phil. I made three suggestions for kids' names in a conference. One – Lucy – survived. The story office came up with Jess and Craig for the other two. It's not an exact science. I often think it's a matter of gut instinct about the feel of a name. Those name discussions can go on for hours. But once the names are in place, the family starts to live.

'As you begin to write, the characters start to appear in your imagination. I know vaguely what they look like but so will all the other writers. Only when we see them for real will we know for sure. At this stage it's more important that they sound right and that means that we all have a clear sense of who they are and what they want so that we can make them speak with a consistent voice.

'As for a favourite character – that's tough. I've written the first two episodes in which they all appear. At this stage I'd opt for Maggie and Jess (Phil's daughter) as being the most clearly defined, although I felt I got a very clear handle on all of them. And that isn't always the case.'

Chris prepared a brief character summary for the new family – an important document. It's not only the basis of the material the team of writers and storyliners will develop for the family, it's the document that the *Soapstars* judges will have in front of them when deciding who should get through:

SOAPSTARS
BIOGRAPHIES AND RELATIONSHIPS

Phil Weston: Has just left his alcoholic wife to come and join Maggie in Emmerdale. The move has been very sudden and he finds himself dealing with a new and unexpected environment. He is awkward with Craig and Lucy, still trying to find his feet in the new family set-up.

Jess Weston: Phil's daughter has been his support for some time as he struggled to deal with her mother. Jess feels guilty about having abandoned her and resents Maggie for finally breaking apart her home. Having acted as a carer for her mother, Jess is mature beyond her years and her relationship with Phil is as an equal. Because of this, she further resents Maggie's treating her as a child. She thinks Lucy is spoiled and is impatient with Craig's laziness.

Maggie Calder: Broke up with her husband some months ago. Her new job in the holiday village is her first since the break-up, and the first assertion of her new independence. Her guilt about the break-up of the marriage has fuelled her over-protectiveness of Lucy. Her relationship with the more mature Craig is less fraught.

Lucy Calder: Is a little spoiled, having been the object of her parents' warring affections. She knows how to manipulate Maggie's feelings of guilt, which infuriates her brother Craig. She is wary of Jess and distrustful of Phil.

Craig Calder: Has provided support to his mother during her break-up. He has a good relationship with her and wants her new life to work out. He has good will towards Phil and is trying to build a relationship with him. He is an appeaser and will do anything for a quiet life. He is impressed by Jess's maturity.

The document is sketchy – that's partly because of the nature of the way this particular family will be cast, but it's also fairly standard practice: the makers want to give firm guidance, but don't want to rule out good actors with too narrow a brief. While the producer and writers have an age range in mind for the characters, everything else is up to who's cast – a good audition might change some of the preconceptions of the character.

Bill Lyons was the *Emmerdale* writer chosen to sit on the *Soapstars* judging panel. He has a clear idea of the brief: 'What we're looking for is a family, mother, father, two daughters and a son. And for the mother and father we're looking for someone in the thirty-five to forty-five age range, which is – in soap terms – leading man/ woman age,' he explains. 'With the kids they're probably going to look between fourteen to nineteen, the three of them. Obviously the two girls – unless they were twins, which is unlikely in this sort of process – are going to be one of fourteen to sixteen and one of nineteen, and the boy is probably eighteen or nineteen.

'We've tried to be a bit flexible and to have room for accommodating someone with particular talent that doesn't necessarily entirely fall into that. Rather than being a standard family that has grown up together, we're going to have two families that come together. Both the husband and wife have come from another marriage, or another relationship, to it. Which will mean that we'll be able to accommodate people with slightly different accents because clearly since we're going all round the country it would be kind of difficult to have a family where we had a Scots, a Midland and a Northern set of children with London parents. We can't accommodate everything but we've tried to be flexible so that we can move with who we've got.

'Obviously in a standard family your three kids would probably speak with the same accent, be the same race. But since we don't know who we're going to find, the possibility is that either the mother or the father may have come from a mixed-race marriage, which will explain why one of the children is Asian when the others aren't, or whatever. So we've tried to leave ourselves room to be able to accommodate the best that we get from this.'

Normally, the character document would go to the casting director of *Emmerdale*, Sue Jackson, who would notify the casting agencies that the show was looking for people to play new regular parts. From this, agents would put forward people that they think would be suitable, and they'd send up CVs and photographs. At this stage, the casting director would select about seven or eight actors, and they'd be called up to Leeds to audition, and be sent the character outline and a short scene to learn. At the audition, the producer, casting director and one of the more experienced *Emmerdale* directors would chat to the actor, then they'd run through the scene. Usually, it would be a two-handed scene and one of the existing cast would play the other part. This cast member will normally be the one who'll be in the most scenes with the new character – if Terry is getting a new girlfriend, then Billy Hartman, who plays Terry, will be the cast member at the audition. The reason is obvious enough – the producer will want the actors to have chemistry together. The established actor will often be asked their opinion.

There are a few other considerations. The casting of British shows isn't quite as formulaic as that in American television, where, for example, if there are three main female characters the network will often insist that there's a blonde, a brunette and a redhead. Where possible, *Emmerdale* will try to avoid casting someone who looks too much like an existing cast member, because it can confuse viewers. Television is a very literal medium – in the theatre, it's possible to cast a thirty-year-old woman as fourteen-year-old Juliet... on television it would almost always look ridiculous. Audiences can accept a certain amount of artistic licence. No one ever seems to worry that many of the characters in *Coronation Street* have Yorkshire accents, or that the Dingles in *Emmerdale* sound like they're from Lancashire.

But the *Emmerdale* office does get a lot of letters complaining about the 'southern accents' of the characters.

The normal audition process for a regular in the series is actually quite a short one, especially for the individual actors. They'll arrive at the *Emmerdale* studio, wait in reception (where they'll probably meet some of the other people who are here for the job), have a brief chat with the producer, then do the scene. The actor will then head back home. The producer usually has a strong gut feeling about who should get the part, but will normally consult a few key people on the programme for a second opinion.

Normally, the decision is made in a couple of days, and the agent of the successful actor is contacted. The actor would normally start within a couple of weeks. *Soapstars*, of course, is a completely different process, especially at first. It's an open audition, advertised in the national press, and in places such as the ITV website. And when news of the audition first got out, it caused more than a few problems....

objections to soapstars

The new series already has its critics. This is emphatically *not* the way that auditions for acting parts are usually held. Almost as soon as *Soapstars* was announced, the press was reporting that the existing cast of *Emmerdale* weren't happy with the idea. Along with other actors and the actors' union, Equity, they have criticized *Soapstars* for trivializing the profession – though this hasn't kept every experienced actor or Equity member away. The *Sun* reported that Malandra Burrows, who played *Emmerdale*'s Kathy Glover, wrote to ITV bosses saying, 'We find this disrespect shattering.' Emily Symons, a veteran of *Home and Away* (where she played

Marilyn), now playing Louise on *Emmerdale*, told the newspaper 'for someone to come along, win a competition and be your equal, it's very difficult'. Jean Rodgers, who played Dolly Skilbeck in *Emmerdale* for eleven years (until 1991), and who is now an Equity Council member, added, 'Most performers are in the business because they want to entertain, inform and enrich the culture of the country, not to be "rich and famous".' On the other hand, Ross Kemp – famous now as Grant Mitchell from *EastEnders*, but who's first soap part was on *Emmerdale* in 1986 as Dolly's secret love child Graham Lodsworth – was far more sympathetic, and was quoted as saying 'Soaps take people who are members of the public anyway. I would suggest that some people from *EastEnders* have no acting experience. If people are good enough to be in a show then they deserve to be in it, and if they are popular with the audience then all credit to them.'

Nigel Jones is the North East Regional Organizer of the actors' union, Equity, who have been vocal in their criticism of *Soapstars*. He explains:

'There were two specific objections which relate to our agreement with the ITV companies and two wider ones. The specifics are that the Agreement lays down minimum terms and payments for the engagement of performers who, among other things, "exercise dramatic skills in plays, features, documentaries, light entertainment, readings and other types of programmes". No payments were initially being proposed for participants who would clearly be obliged to "exercise dramatic skills" for the camera.

'Secondly, under the Agreement the ITV companies' declared policy is to offer engagements "to experienced professional performers". The whole point of *Soapstars* was to put individuals into a soap (which turned out to be *Emmerdale*) who in all likelihood would not be professionals. This is hard to take when a high proportion of experienced artists are out of work.

'The other considerations were in respect of the profession as a whole which many observers (and not just among actors and those within Equity) felt was demeaned by the notion that a much sought-after job should be offered as a competition prize, like a weekend break in Torquay! As Andrew Collins wrote in the *Observer*, "it trivialises what an actor does to say that anyone can do it."

'The Equity Council issued a press release which condemned *Soapstars* as "an insulting affront to the men and women in our profession who endure low rates of pay, rejection and humiliation in the course of their work, despite their training, experience, dedication and talent". Colin Tarrant, a Council member who plays Inspector Monroe in *The Bill*, added, "This docusoap encourages stereotypical misconceptions about the profession and exploits them in order to create cheap, sensational, publicity-seeking television and therefore, on behalf of our membership, must be condemned."

'The final consideration was in respect of the existing cast of *Emmerdale*. When it became clear that this was the show chosen, our members on the show reacted with alarm. They wrote to Equity and the producers saying "*Soapstars* is a rotten idea." They were concerned that their privacy would be compromised with *Soapstars* cameras following them into the green room and the bathroom, and felt undermined by the notion that the first rate show they strive tirelessly to produce should be entrusted to people who had simply won a competition. As their letter put it, it was as though in their "training and many years of experience in theatre and television (we) have been wasting our time." And, not least, it was by no means clear at the outset that they would be paid for the contributions to *Soapstars* they would be expected to make.

'Some of these specific concerns have been addressed, but in our view the programme remains ill-conceived and damaging to the acting profession and the TV industry.

'We could have instructed our membership not to participate as auditionees; we could have instructed our members in *Emmerdale* to refuse to co-operate with the *Soapstars* process because of the *prima facie* breaches of the Agreement. After the producers offered various safeguards and concessions our Council opted not to do this while making clear that opposition to the concept of the show remained very strong.

'Our discussions with the producers resulted in payments under the Equity/ITV Agreement to all participants who progressed beyond the mass audition stage. But while it is true that these discussions took place and payments resulted from them, our Council felt unable to make a formal agreement with the producers due to our objection in principle to the whole concept of the programme.

'We have however reached agreement over the financial basis for the participation of the current *Emmerdale* cast pursuant to the Equity/ITV Agreement, and also upon the question of the cast's right to privacy and right not to be involved in interviews etc, except on a voluntary basis.

'The fifteen-second stage should not be brushed aside. It really was tawdry. But the rest of the process differed from a "real" audition in that the *Soapstars* auditions were being filmed for mass consumption. This is hardly a semantic distinction! It put extra pressure on the auditionees to know that their mistakes would be witnessed by millions and that they risked public humiliation. Actors have to live with rejection, but it is normally a private process, not one to spice up other people's prime-time viewing! And a "normal" audition would be founded on the knowledge that the auditionees are professional performers who can act: they wouldn't expect to be put through exercises to see if they can act or not! That was clearly still happening after the fifteen-second stage.

'These participants were principally seeking a part in a soap, not to have their lives charted. This is the crux: the casting process was a secondary consideration against the imperative of creating cheap easy-consumption TV. We do not believe that the charting of one's professional life – rejection and all – should be a condition of being allowed to audition for any part.

'We issued no instruction to members not to participate (although we did nothing to encourage them either) and certainly would not take any action against them. We'd be pleased to see professionals coming out on top.

'Our argument was never with the participants. If any of them are not existing members of Equity, they will be encouraged to join. There is, and has always been, provision under our agreements to bring in newcomers, which is clearly essential to replenish the profession. But this is not the way we would have chosen to do it.'

Steve Frost acknowledges there was some tension. 'There was concern that we would introduce five "non-actors" to the cast, but that was clearly not what we intended. The process was long and rigorous and the five people chosen had to prove repeatedly that they were capable and deserving of a part. I think the cast were satisfied that *Emmerdale* would keep control of the process and would not be forced to take actors chosen by other people and not approved by ourselves. It was not a case of *Emmerdale* accommodating five "competition winners", but of us choosing, through a long and televised but otherwise fairly standard procedure, five actors who we wanted in the programme.'

It's a question that worries the hopefuls – most understand why the existing cast members might be wary. One of the semi-finalists, Mark Satchell, complains about the publicity for the show: 'It was all "Do you want to be famous?" and "So you want to be the star of a soap?" That's not right. It should have been "Are you *good enough* to be the star of a soap?"'

Much of the initial publicity, and the first few shows, concentrates on the crowds and the people who made a fool of themselves at the initial fifteen-second audition stage. It's not clear from the pre-publicity that, once past the open auditions, the hopefuls will be reading scenes and giving a more direct demonstration of acting skills and techniques. Later in the process, those that get through will have question-and-answer sessions with a couple of

Emmerdale actors, Lisa Riley and Patrick Mower, and both will say almost exactly the same thing: they stress that *Emmerdale* is a friendly place, but that will change for the Soapstars if they aren't up to the job, if they don't know their lines or can't hit their marks.

Soapstars producer Tim Miller stresses that it's an open audition, which means that actors are welcome, and also that the parts aren't going to be won in a game show: 'We are looking for new talent, but that doesn't mean that we're excluding people with acting experience. All the finalists of *Popstars* had some background in singing. We have to look for a number of things as well as checking that people can act. We have to ask if they can learn their lines quickly, can they work well as a team and how do they look on camera? I think we will show how getting a part in a soap is a long and very hard process and not everyone can do it. We will probably see a lot of talent being lost along the way.'

So, *Soapstars* was on. Tim Miller had the task of coming up with a format that would square the circle of making an entertaining programme, while also giving *Emmerdale* five good actors. 'Dreaming up what we would get people to do was very much a team effort,' he says. 'I wrote up a basic game-plan, but it was very much a working document. Researchers and directors threw in their ideas and I also spoke to one of the main producers on *Popstars*, who had his own ideas on how we could make it work.

'Crucially, we had to ensure that at each stage the process moved on. First, the fifteen seconds, then the *Emmerdale* scenes, then the screen test. At the semi-finals, there was the kissing, then the famous scenes from *Coronation Street*, the line-learning test and finally the actual scenes for the new *Soapstars* family. At the finals, the producers arrived, then there was the screen coach, then the scenes on location, the trip to *Emmerdale*, the scenes with Patrick Mower, etc.'

It was essential that there was plenty of variety on offer to grab viewers from the very start. 'We would not have established the hopefuls as people at that stage, so it was important that the audition material was intrinsically entertaining,' Tim explains. 'This is one of the reasons for those fifteen-second auditions – another was the need to get through thousands of people as quickly as possible!

'As well as variety, we needed to ensure that the viewers could compare like with like – and this is why we made people do the same scenes,' Tim adds. 'By cutting these scenes back to back, it would highlight the very, very good and the very, very bad. This is also why we cut in the scenes with real *Emmerdale* footage. This served as a reference point. I think this was vital, because acting is more subtle than singing. Viewers would need to be given a steer in who could do it and who couldn't.'

Keith Richardson believes that despite the unique opportunity offered to aspiring actors by *Soapstars*, the eventual winners will be under no less pressure to perform than any other actor. 'I expect most of the people that make it past the opening stages are going to be actors already. If they are adults they'll have acted in the past and were forced to give it up for family or income reasons. They've reached the stage where they want to try acting again, they're more settled or whatever. It's a way of getting on without having a posh agent, and we've seen that there's a lot of talent out there that normally doesn't get a chance.'

That said, Keith is quick to stress the realities of being a jobbing soap actor: 'You need dedication to be an actor, you have to experience scrutiny and rejection. There's a belief that soap acting is somehow secondary to "real" acting. I hope that this programme shows just how wrong that is – there are long hours, a lot of lines to learn, it's hard work.' He is confident that the new family will work well in *Emmerdale*, but is quite blunt about what will happen if, for whatever reason, things don't pan out as planned: 'They're in exactly the same position as any other actor under contract. There's no pressure to keep them in because they're the winners of *Soapstars*. If they're not up to the job, they won't get any favours.'

the panellists

A crucial early decision was selecting a panel of three judges. They had to embody the two jobs *Soapstars* set out to do – the programme will stand or fall on them being entertaining to watch, while also being expert enough to pick the right five people. Tim Miller: 'The judges were chosen by myself and my executive producer, Natalka Znak. But we worked in consultation with Keith, Steve and the Network Centre.

'Paul de Freitas was suggested by Keith,' Tim says. 'Natalka and I paid him a visit and were immediately convinced that we should build our panel around him. He was clearly keen to take part and we thought his camp wit would make good TV. After attending the writers' meeting, I picked out Bill. He'd had a bit of a heated debate with someone at the meeting. We were obviously looking for someone with strong opinions and someone who was passionate about *Emmerdale*. Bill scored on both counts. We guessed his gruff, cynical image would contrast nicely with Paul's camp nature.

'We thought we should have a woman as the third panel member and spent a long time looking. We met TV writers, drama tutors, talked to agents about former soap actresses. In the end, it was Keith who suggested Yvon. The moment she waltzed in to our office we knew she was the one. Very opinionated and feisty.'

PAUL DE FREITAS is a casting director. He studied to be an actor, and was in Alan Parker's *Bugsy Malone*. His first job in television was presenting a cookery programme for LWT with Nanette Newman. Now he runs a casting agency, and has worked on a number of prominent advertising campaigns, including Carling Black Label, McDonald's, Lloyds Bank and Kraft Philadelphia. He also directed a Kelloggs Fruit 'N' Fibre advert that was Ross Kemp's first TV work, and other discoveries include Liz Hurley, Catherine Zeta Jones, Minnie Driver and Jude Law. Earlier this year, a Party Election Broadcast he directed for the Conservative Party about asylum seekers was pulled at the last minute due to a political controversy. Paul has recently become a committee member of the Casting Directors' Guild.

What will Paul bring to the *Soapstars* process? 'Being a casting director, which I've been for over twenty years now, I've cast lots of television commercials, absolutely thousands of them,' he explains. 'I've done the occasional film and television series as well along the way and I get to meet lots of young and interesting – and several old and interesting – people who are looking for parts in television, a break, an opportunity. And it's my job really to spot them early on and try to give them that break and that opportunity…. I've done that many times and many people that I've actually spotted in the early stages of their career are currently in soaps or have been in soaps or have gone on to other things as well.'

And what is Paul on the lookout for? 'An original talent. Sometimes a unique personality, people that aren't always brilliant actors and actresses but actually have a sort of character of their own that they can bring to a soap or a commercial or a film or whatever I might be working on. But primarily, talent does help at the end of it all!'

BILL LYONS is a script writer for *Emmerdale,* and has spent forty years working in television – not just writing, but directing, devising, script editing, storylining, even working as an assistant floor manager. He started out as an actor, and appeared in a number of soaps and other shows in the early Sixties – at a time when they went out live. These included *Dixon of Dock Green, Coronation Street* and *Z Cars.* Bill was starting to dabble with writing, and his first radio play was heard by the *Z Cars* producer, Ron Craddock, who recognized Bill's name and asked him to write for the series. From there, he's become one of the most prolific writers on British television. He's written episodes for series such as *Angels, Juliet Bravo* and *Blake's 7,* and a number of one-off plays (including *One Third of the Wise Men,* about his father, Lord Lyons, a long-term advisor of Harold Wilson). However, Bill has made a career writing for soaps, including the original *Crossroads* and the formative years of *EastEnders.* Since 1983 he's been a stalwart of *Emmerdale.*

In 1990, he took what turned out to be a brief break from *Emmerdale* to work on another soap: '*Eldorado* – well, most people don't talk about it but I do... it's the only show that I've ever worked on that hasn't been a major success. Funnily enough, I believe that there were some very good scripts. At the risk of being shot, I thought the acting and the casting was pretty poor. The technical difficulty of working in another country and being thrown out into the world in Spain was quite a shock really.'

So what does Bill hope to bring to *Soapstars*? 'Well, as a writer on the show, I think I've got probably a different view from the others. I mean, firstly I've got to work with these people. So we can certainly make a mistake, but if we do I'm the one that's got to live with it, nobody else on the panel has to. I'm the one that's gonna eat with them in the canteen and I'm the one that's gonna see them destroy my beautiful words if they're no good....

'What will probably happen is the public will watch and think someone can do something quite well and maybe I won't be that interested, because any character in a long-running soap has to have a fairly wide range. We've got excellent character actors in the show but some maybe won't be able to carry a certain sort of story – it's not their job to do so. But what we're looking for at the moment is more people that can carry quite a wide range of stories. Particularly if you look at the kids, they're an unwritten page. And if they can just do one thing, they're not really a lot of use in a long-running show.

'We want people with a bit of potential. They need to think that their character is someone that you want to follow, as they grew up, got the first job, got the first love... well, maybe not the first love these days if you're taking them on at nineteen. Probably their nineteenth love, but the first one that we've actually seen....

'It's a really hungry machine, a five-times-a-week soap. Whether as a writer or anyone else that's actually working on it, you realize the amount of material that's devoured in such a short time, which is why I really am probably more seriously looking at whether these people can do lots of different things within it.'

YVON GRACE is a TV producer. She was an actress for four years, before becoming a script editor on *EastEnders* and then the producer of *Holby City*. She's also worked on *The Ward* and *My Dad's a Boring Nerd*, which won the British Comedy Award for Children's Comedy Drama in 1997.

Why have a producer on the panel? 'I hope I'm bringing twelve years' experience in casting, in working with people, in managing people, in picking out potential, bringing people on, encouraging talent, being able to focus on the thing that person has got and bringing it out of them. I see myself as very much an initiator. I like to get the right people around me, who are the best at their job, and then let them do it. That's how I see good management and also how I see good production.

'What I love about the potential of this *Soapstars* idea is that there will be people who we put on camera, who have never, ever done it before. And if they get through – if they get through to even the semis – it will validate the whole process for me. It's giving people that chance that they never had before. And if I can see that talent in them, and bring them through the whole process, and hopefully give them encouragement along the way, then that's a good producer thing to do. It will be nerve-wracking and their confidence may fail, but I want to be there to make sure that doesn't happen. That's part of what I do as a producer.'

'A writer, obviously, is an essential part of the whole process, because without the script there wouldn't be any acting. But it's not very often a writer gets the chance to

PAUL DE FREITAS, panellist

'I speak my mind, if people are late I get annoyed. But I certainly hope that people don't think that I'm the next Nasty Nigel.'

sit in on a casting session, or to choose the actors he or she writes for. A casting director does specifically that – nothing else – in the drama process. A producer, if they're worth their salt, in my view, not only initiates the script but develops the script from the storyline to script with the writer. They also then, having created the script that they're going to be needing actors for, cast it. They also then choose a director who is going to bring the whole thing together. And the cameraman, and the sound man. So a producer has the overall experience of making drama happen.'

The judges ponder their alliterative nicknames. If *Popstars* had 'Nasty Nigel', then what will *Soapstars* have?

'Hopefully I won't be Bored Bill.'

'I wanted to be Yummy Yvon, but people are already talking about Viper Yvon, or Evil Yvon. It's better than Bland Yvon, isn't it?'

Paul's pleased when the crowds outside shout, 'Pick me, Paul!', but isn't keen on getting a nickname: 'I think if they applied that sort of "Nasty" title to me it would be very unfair…. I'm just honest and it's an honest business. I didn't even think Nigel Lithgow was that nasty….

'I think it's a very tough business, people speak their mind – read any of the reviews of the critics when they're reviewing programmes, when they're reviewing the theatre…. But at the same time, I'm not turning up to these places to annihilate the locals and be vicious and nasty to them. That's not what the spirit of this programme is about and it's not how I conduct myself in my professional career.'

emmerdale: behind the cameras

Names and job titles scroll past in the credits at the end of every programme, but it's not always obvious who does what, or what the difference between a production co-ordinator, assistant producer, production assistant, line producer, producer or an executive producer is. To list everyone who worked on a soap and to give a detailed description of everything they did in their jobs would take a whole book, but it's possible to concentrate on a few of the more important roles.

THE PRODUCER
Every television programme has a producer. In the movies, the producer is the person who buys a script and secures financial backing from a studio – they're in charge of the financial and administrative aspects of the film. In television, the role is different – producers are under contract to a television production company (in *Emmerdale*'s case, YTV), usually stay on a programme for two or three years, and they are the person who is in complete and overall charge of the series. They have the final say on the artistic direction, casting, approving scripts and appointing staff, so it's a time-consuming, demanding job. The current producer of *Emmerdale* is Steve Frost, who's been in the job for almost a year.

Soapstars has its own producer, Tim Miller, who's been the series producer for *Airline, Britain's Most Wanted* and *For*

Better For Worse. Before then, he'd worked on a number of LWT factual programmes; he originally started out as a journalist on the *Eastern Daily Press.* How did he get the *Soapstars* job? 'I was series producing *Airline* (another LWT production) and was taken off it early to work on *Soapstars.* Because I'm employed by LWT rather than freelance, I basically have to do what I'm told. But they do give you some choice in what projects you want to work on and, obviously, I wasn't going to turn down *Soapstars.*

'Frankly, at first I was terrified!' he confesses. '*Popstars* was absolutely huge and so it was going to be a tough act to follow. But it was also extremely exciting to be working on such a high-profile project.'

THE WRITER

On some shows, different writers will collaborate on scripting, writing different story threads, concentrating on one set of characters, perhaps playing to their individual strengths. *Emmerdale* uses the system that's more usual in British television – one writer is responsible for each script.

On *Emmerdale*, there is a pool of about twenty writers, each of whom can write around a dozen scripts a year. *Emmerdale* writers aren't allowed to work on other soaps while they're working on *Emmerdale*, but – if they've got time or the inclination – they can do other writing work. One of the judges of *Soapstars*, Bill Lyons, is the longest-serving writer on *Emmerdale*. Another writer, Chris Thompson, outlined the five characters that the *Soapstars* winners will play (and wrote the first episode they will appear in); and another, Karin Young, is writing the script for the video that will feature them. Writers on a soap take sole credit for the scripts they write, but they don't work in complete isolation, or just come up with the stories off their own bat. The writers all meet every three weeks for a story conference with the producer, where they compare notes on the latest storylines and discuss the future of the series. Also there are:

THE STORY EDITOR AND STORYLINERS

Before a script is written, a small team of people, overseen by the story editor, co-ordinates the detail of the stories, to make sure every story is being told at the right pace and that no important beats are left out, or repeated. The storyliners draw up detailed documents for the writers, spelling out exactly what happens in each episode and which stories are the most important. They take into account practical issues – such as trying to balance out studio and location work. They also check cast availability – making sure that a character isn't in an episode if the actor is on holiday, making sure all the cast have enough to do, without overloading anyone's schedule. Storylines are done in a block of fifteen every three weeks, with the latest batch being the first order of business at every story conference.

THE SCRIPT EDITOR

Once the writer has written a script, it goes to a script editor. The script editor checks the script to make sure it's not too long or too short (every *Emmerdale* script has to be twenty-three and a half minutes, give or take a few seconds), all the story points have been included, and that it doesn't contradict the other scripts around it or anything else established in the past of the show.

The script editor suggests improvements to the writers – typically to make the 'sting' for the ad break more exciting, or to build on scripts that the writer may not have seen, because they were being written at the same time he was writing. Because there are so many scripts in production at any one time, *Emmerdale* has two script editors – these are Karen Grimes and Katie Swinden.

Once a script has been approved by the script editor and producer, it goes to…

THE DIRECTOR

The director is responsible for carrying out a successful recording of an episode, for turning a script into a piece of television. On *Emmerdale*, directors now work in 'blocks' of five episodes at a time. The directors are freelance, and (hopefully!) work on many other programmes during the course of a year. *Emmerdale* uses a pool of directors who can end up doing as many as half a dozen blocks a year. It's the director who's in charge on the studio floor or on location – he's the one that tells the actors, cameramen, lighting men, sound men and so on what to do.

Directors can bring a distinctive look and pace to an episode – even on *Emmerdale*, where they are all working with the same sets, locations, cast and crew. On *Emmerdale*, obviously most of the cast are regulars, but directors do have some say in casting, particularly for characters that only appear in their episodes. Because of the hectic schedule, there are two units working at any given time – two directors, working on their separate episodes.

A director also supervises the editing of an episode, working with…

THE EDITOR

After the video footage has been recorded, the editor assembles it, selecting the best shots to tell the story.

Working with the director, the editor chooses (from the available tapes) the best shots to start and end scenes with, and decides which actors will be in shot. On *Emmerdale*, the studio footage is actually edited together as it's recorded, to save time – this 'live' editing is done in the studio control room, or gallery, by a vision mixer. Location footage, including the scenes recorded in the village, is edited later.

These days, virtually all television editing is done on computer – both *Emmerdale* and *Soapstars* use a system called Avid, the software that is pretty much the industry standard. The *Emmerdale* studio is self-contained – it has its own editing suites. The *Soapstars* office has three editing suites of its own.

THE LINE PRODUCER

'Line producer' is a term that can mean different things on different series. On *Emmerdale*, there is one line producer, Tim Fee. Since 1988, Tim has been responsible for solving the logistic challenges of making *Emmerdale*. It's at least a full-time job to make sure that the scripts can be made into television on a tight budget, not to mention making sure that the fifty cast members and a hundred crew members know where they ought to be, when they ought to be there, and how they'll get to the right place in time.

Tim's job also includes managing the studio and village sites – and they are, respectively, the largest television studio and permanent outdoor set in the world!

soapstars: behind the cameras

As well as judges, Tim Miller also assembled his production crew. As he explains:

ALICE MAYHALL, researcher

'By the end we had got to know the people really well. It was quite hard for us when they were rejected. At the semi-finals many of the production team were in tears.'

RESEARCHERS – Senti Mukasa and Alice Mayhall

'Their job was to help find the venues, track down scripts for the auditions, shoot material on DV at the auditions. But most crucial of all was the logging. We shot about 700 tapes in total. The directors needed some way of finding the good bits quickly. So the researchers spent their time religiously noting down the "time-codes" so that the material could be accessed quickly. They put together packages of the highlights that the directors could dip into. The other crucial bit of the job was to get to know the hopefuls and interview them.

'As well as his other responsibilities, Senti had a specific brief to look after the panel. He would drive them to the auditions, drive them back, drop them off at the station and generally keep them happy. Someone had to do it....'

ASSISTANT RESEARCHER – Tom Whitrow

'Tom's main job was to sort out all the scripts for the auditions. He then manned the call-back table where the winners came to collect their scripts. Back at the office he helped out with the logging.'

PRODUCTION ASSISTANT – Marnie Sirota

'Marnie's main job was to log the material being shot by the Digi-BETA crews at the auditions. She wrote down the badge number, the time-code, a description of the audition and –

MARNIE SIROTA, production assistant

'I was always in the thick of the auditions and had a good steer on who would be picked. Because my headphones picked up everything the panel said, I felt I was a real insider.'

crucially – noted the comments made by the panel. When she got back to the office, she typed up all the logs, masterminded an administrative system for tapes and for writing up logs that enabled directors to track down material in minutes. As the programmes get close to transmission, Marnie has been checking for commercial references, music clearance, archive clearance.'

ASSISTANT PRODUCERS – Sharon Walker and Caroline Morris

'They shot on DV at the auditions. Interviewing people about how it was going, looking for interesting stories and characters. Much of the material in the programmes came from these interviews rather than the auditions themselves.'

PRODUCTION CO-ORDINATOR – Yvonne James

'If it all goes wrong in TV, Yvonne says she's guaranteed a job in a travel agency. She masterminded the smooth

SHARON WALKER, assistant producer

'The auditions were incredibly hard. We would be up at 5.30am putting out cones and filming the queues. We'd finish at about 6pm, but then we had to pack up and there would be a briefing in the bar at about 8pm.'

movement of around thirty production crew. From the panel to the punters, Yvonne made it happen. Hotels, trains, planes and automobiles. At the semi-finals, Yvonne took charge of making sure all the hopefuls got down to London safely. She was coordinating travel from as far afield as Barcelona to Bradford.

'The other main job was to oversee the "call-sheets", the bible that the production team uses on a shoot to know who should be where at what time. There were around thirty names on one of our call-sheets. Inside would be details of where all thirty should be at what time. Without Yvonne nothing would happen.

'But there was a less glamorous side to her job. She was the one who wrote the numbers on the badges.'

PRODUCTION MANAGER – Malcolm Donkin

'He became a bit of a cult figure with the auditionees after making a name for himself with his health and safety talks. No one was interested, but Malcolm always got a big clap.

'Malcolm is the money-man who keeps an eye on the budget and tells me what I can and can't spend. He negotiates all the deals with the venues, the cameramen, the graphics team, and of course the panel. He also has a responsibility for health and safety and security. At each venue we would hire about ten security staff to cope with the large numbers of people. He would liaise with the local police and the local councils to make sure that everyone was happy with what was planned.

'His other crucial job was to plan the schedule, to book all the editors, etc. Because he was also doing *Soapstars Extra* [the extended one-hour version on ITV2], it was a massive job.'

PRODUCER/DIRECTORS – **Jo Scarratt, Putul Verma, Toby Faulkner, Carolyn Payne, Dave Sayer, Heather Nash**
'Their job was to cut each programme. Each stage of the finals would have a different director. For the first programme (an hour) the directors were given five weeks. The next programmes all had three weeks. But the directors at the finals each had little more than a week, because we were shooting the material so close to transmission.'

RUNNERS – **Vikki Minchin and Celia Dean**
'University students who helped out at the auditions – ferrying people around, getting tea and coffee, water for crew and panel. Helped with photocopying forms, badges, etc.'

CREW
'At the regionals we had three Digi Beta crews, all with a cameraman and a sound recordist. From the second day of the semis onwards, we cut that down to two. Under the direction of the director, they lit the venues and shot the material on stage and backstage with the panel. The material was beamed on to a monitor by radio link and the director was able to chat to the crews through their ear-pieces.'

So, with the format and personnel in place, all they needed now were the hopefuls....

famous for fifteen seconds

CHAPTER TWO

Friday 8 June to Sunday 8 July, 2001.
The open auditions – 5,000 become sixty-four.

The makers of *Soapstars* assumed there would be a good response to the adverts, and they weren't disappointed. There were five open regional auditions planned – and a huge number of people turned up, the approximate numbers being:

Sheffield – 1,000
Bristol – 500
Birmingham – 1,000
Glasgow – 400
London – 2,000

So, nearly 5,000 people at this stage. And the crowds arrive early – every venue sees at least one person who has slept overnight to guarantee an early audition. In London, there were several dozen camping out, and many hundreds more turning up before the film crews did at eight in the morning.

Producer Tim Miller had to plan for this: 'We had no idea what to expect. We were actually quite concerned about it because we knew that we couldn't physically see more than a thousand in one day. In London we were able to increase the numbers by splitting the panel. That didn't work as well for us, as we missed out on the panel dynamic but at least we got through more people. We still had to tell some that they wouldn't be seen and it wasn't a pleasant job.'

Not everyone who turns up qualifies. For a start, the actors have to be over sixteen. Child actors have restrictions on their working hours, and there are a number of other serious legal ramifications. This age restriction is made clear in all the adverts and publicity that goes out, but many under-sixteens do show up, and often resent being sent straight home. The judges also spot a couple of people who've lied about their age.

While the casting brief is as vague as it can be, *Emmerdale* are looking for a mum, a dad and three teenaged kids. Anyone who looks more than about fifty is almost certainly out of the running. But just about everyone who looks like they're in their twenties and early thirties are, too. As it happens, a lot of the people that get through are in their twenties, but look either younger or older. But a lot of the people in their late twenties who look their age are disappointed, and grumble about 'restrictions'.

They can also only see a thousand people a day. It means all-day queues for a lot of people. It means that some people

---

TIM MILLER, *Soapstars* producer

'We employed security and ushers at each venue. But in London we had people climbing under gates and on to roofs etc. People without badges were getting them off people who'd just been rejected.'

won't be seen at all. Members of the production team, sometimes even the judges, go to the back of the queue and warn the people there they probably won't be seen, unless a lot of people drop out. Mark Jardine is one of the people at Sheffield who takes the hint:

'They said they probably wouldn't see me, and that if they did it would be about four in the afternoon. That was at about nine o'clock. So I took the hint and went home.'

Dean Abrahams is a bit more cocky. He persuades Paul that he should jump the queue. Paul obviously doesn't want to turn anyone away with potential, and he's gone down the line picking out a few girls and boys. Dean Abrahams takes some of the initiative for himself, practically leaping out and asking Paul to select him.

There are also some touching moments – one of the girls, Jade, meets her childhood sweetheart Will in the queue, and they go in together. Both get through the fifteen second stage – Jade falls at the next hurdle, Will lasts until day three.

Most of the people who've turned up are ushered inside, about two dozen at a time. There they are given badges with a number on, a form to fill in with their name and address, and a legal release to sign, which grants *Soapstars* the rights to film them and use the results on television (and in this book).

The hopefuls are led into the hall and faced with a large stage with the three judges sitting behind a table. They take their seats, and stare up at the judges, trying to suss out what they are looking for. A lot of the hopefuls think the judges look pretty outlandish – Paul's colourful suits, Yvon's shock of hair, Bill Lyons' expression practically defining 'lugubrious'. It's often hard to hear what the hopefuls trooping up onto the stage are saying, but it's very obvious that the judges are dismissing people extremely fast – many aren't even getting the full fifteen seconds – and that barely a handful are getting through. The panel make Nasty Nigel look like he was dawdling. This isn't going to be easy.

For most people, there's a long wait, followed by instant disappointment. For others, there's success – Jo-Ann D'Costa recovers from a poor start, telling the judges she's good, rather than demonstrating it. But she improvises a scene and gets through. As the camera follows her off the stage, she's plays up to it, giving a broad grin.

This isn't just an audition – Tim Miller has a programme to make. He's sent Sharon Walker out with a smaller camera on her shoulder to record scenes of the crowd, to see people rehearsing and in the hall, waiting for their turn, listening to the competition. At each venue there's a photographer taking shots of proceedings, from pictures of individuals to shots of the queues outside and the groups inside. Tim co-ordinates it all from a desk at the foot of the stage, with production assistant Marnie Sirota, who keeps a close eye on the monitor to make sure the pictures serve their two purposes – to give a good record of the performances, and that they're collecting entertaining footage they can use on *Soapstars*.

No one turning up really knows what is expected of them, but again this has been carefully devised. Yvon explains the structure for the open auditions: 'Stage one is fifteen seconds – they've got fifteen seconds to impress the judges. Getting through will be tough but when they do they go in to stage two, which is when they get to do proper scenes that have been written specifically for *Emmerdale* and they get to work with these scenes on camera. Which is a very good test.

'Then, hearts in their mouths, they'll be waiting – have they got through to stage three? If they have they get called back on the third day and we improvise with them... this is where we don't give them anything to do at all apart from prepare natural scenes in situ in another venue and we film that process. And having got through that one, if they get through we get to the fourth stage, which is where we put them on camera and test what they look like on camera. And the gruelling thing for that person would be if they got through all those stages, and they failed the screen test, because there's nothing they can do about that, it's just if the camera does them justice or makes them look too young or too old or whatever, we can't do anything about it. But they've gone all the way through those stages so it's really specifically worked out to test at every stage the nerve of the contestant as much as anything.'

With so many people to see, the first part of the process is probably the hardest of all. It's certainly the one with the worst odds for success. The candidates are told to be original. The idea is not that the hopefuls recite a poem or monologue, but that they show some improvisational skill, and some presence as actors. The sensible ones will remember that they are here for a role in a soap – it's the one question the judges are asking at this stage: 'Is there any hope they're right for the part?'

The makers admit that the fifteen-second audition is a necessary evil – they have to have some way of quickly reducing the numbers to manageable levels. Tim Miller: 'The fifteen-second idea came jointly from me and *Popstars* producer James Breen.

'It wasn't a very accurate way of working out who was good and who wasn't. But it was a way of seeing a lot of

TIM MILLER, *Soapstars* producer

'We employed security and ushers at each venue. But in London we had people climbing under gates and on to roofs, etc. People without badges were getting them off people who'd just been rejected.'

people very quickly. The idea was to use it as an initial filter to get people with the right look and then to test their acting ability at stage two.

'It generated a bit of publicity, but anyone who's seen the programme would realize that the fifteen-second auditions made up only part of programme one and part of programme two. There was much, much more to the *Soapstars* audition process.'

And what would Tim have done for his fifteen seconds?

'Undoubtedly, I would have been a shouter and, undoubtedly, I would have been rejected very, very quickly.'

Bill Lyons is under no illusions as to the downsides to the fifteen-second audition. 'If John Gielgud came up, there's no guarantee that in fifteen seconds you would realize he was a great actor. I mean, how are you going to do that? So you've just got to look for any spark, any clue. Somebody that does something terribly original, even if it's something that you can't use, is probably worth a second go because you think, "Well, if they've had the brightness to work out that they're gonna do something different from a thousand other people, they've probably got a spark of something in there...."'

Paul's optimistic about what the lightning-fast auditions may reveal: 'I think they're going to have to come on, really impress us, do something that makes the three of us look at one another and say, "Yeah, let's give them another chance

PAUL DE FREITAS, panellist

'You know, I've got lists of people who are now very famous people that came in for me and spent more than fifteen seconds and didn't get anywhere at that particular time. It's just the right thing happening at the right time for people. It works for some and it doesn't for others.'

and get them through to the next stage because we want to spend more time with them." And I'm all for giving people an opportunity to prove themselves. If they look right and they've got something a little bit imaginative and original, then I'll give them a chance to come back. I'm not saying we're going to come up and rush forward with a contract but I'd be interested in spending more time with them....

'One of my concerns about doing this process of giving people fifteen seconds is that people will slip through the net – good people will. And that is inevitable. We'll do our best to have that avoided but it does happen in the casting world.'

So, if you want to impress the judges, what should you do? Yvon's got some tips: 'The person that gets through will be somebody that is completely conscious of who they are. There's no point in just standing in front of us and going "er... " – you've already wasted three seconds of the fifteen you've got! This is your chance!

'I think they should prepare fifteen seconds of something. I think that it's going to be really difficult for them because a lot of people will never have done that before – I mean, I certainly haven't done it before, but if someone said to me, "What would you do, Yvon?", I would say, "Oh, you know, I'll tell them about the time that me and me Nanna hitchhiked across Ireland." I won't get very far through that story, but it's about the funniest thing I've ever done. And because I could say that with conviction, the person listening will believe me. They have to just make me believe in what they're saying. It's a hard thing to do, almost impossible, but I'm sure it will happen.

'The first thing they've got to face is a heck of a lot of exposure from the people that are watching, because the other auditionees will be in the auditorium as well, and then they've got to face the three of us and I have a feeling that actually we're probably quite scary en masse, the three of us sitting there. They've also got to have an awful lot of self-belief in order to get through that fifteen seconds.'

Ruth Abram is in the first group of people at the very first audition in Sheffield. She doesn't even need the full fifteen seconds – she steps up onto the stage carrying a plastic bag, introduces herself and is about to explain what's in the bag, but Yvon tells her she's through. The process has taken eight seconds. Ruth says there have been worse examples at open auditions – she went to an open casting call for a teen soap, and the first stage of that simply consisted of walking past the judges without saying a word.

There are a few people who might have fared better under that system. Kimberley, a striking red-haired girl in a white dress at the Birmingham audition, goes for an over-wrought emotional crying scene – the judges aren't convinced. Yvon singles it out as a common fault on the

---

YVON GRACE, panellist

'I bet sometimes it'll be the longest fifteen seconds in some people's lives. And other times it'll be the longest in my life, but I think that's what I'm looking for. If they don't have that self-belief you can see it, and the fifteen seconds will bring that out.'

day: 'Crying. Miserable people do not work. When we've seen a thousand miserable people, we all want to just cut our wrists and go home.'

The judges dismiss Kimberley, unconvinced by her tears – and a moment later, Kimberley is at the side of the hall, crying for real this time, and being comforted by a friend. The judges still aren't impressed. 'I think it was because of my hair,' Kimberley tells a member of the camera crew.

A couple of months later, the day after the first episode of *Soapstars* (which includes Kimberley's performance) is broadcast, the *Soapstars* website goes active, and a message board allows people to post their reactions and comments. Kimberley herself is one of the first to contribute. And she's got a lot to get off her chest:

Ok, I agree, I know the business is harsh, I have been doing it for a few years now, but however many rejections I have had, I can't remember a single one that has been so blatantly nasty. It's not a case of not 'liking her', or being put off by her comments, becuase I have had plenty of put downs in my time. I just think that the media has taken it too far. Basically, it's really unprofessional. Did you know that Soapstars wasn't going to be aired, because the professional people at Equity and from other soaps as well as Emmerdale were protesting about 'wannabes' with no professional training or experience could win a place in a soap. Heres a analogy for you:

DOCTORSTARS: *Win a place at a top London hospital by auditioning. You have 15 seconds to prove you are a good doctor. No experience or training needed.*

If this was true, there would be outrage. Don't you think that Soapstars is exactly the same? I know I auditioned, and yes, I may have made a bit of a prat of myself, and yes, I may be a bit overdramatic, but that, I feel is my personality. People that hide their emotions become serial killers. (no kidding)

I auditioned for the experience, and I got very intense about it. Thats the way I like to work.

I say, 'Well, I have to move on. It's their problem if I wasn't picked, and if I have to wait a million years for a part and fame I will.' It's what I want to do, and nothing will stand in the way of my dream. (I just quit a really prestigious school because I got a substantial filmimg role, and they wouldn't let me do it.) That is how dedicated I am.

I know that someday I will get a proper chance. I will wait for that day.

A clip of Kimberley from the first episode is shown that night on *This Week Only*, as part of a short item on *Soapstars*. The presenters aren't impressed.

People adopt a number of approaches to try to get themselves noticed by the judges. The most obvious one is also the least likely to succeed – making a fool of yourself. At Birmingham, Pauline steps on to the stage swathed in bandages, saying she heard the panel was on the lookout for a soap mummy. She's swiftly rejected, although in her case, Paul has a change of heart: 'We told her to go and get changed because we wanted to be able to see her properly. She said, "I came on the bus like this!", but she ran out, borrowed somebody else's clothes, got changed, and came back in again."

The camera teams pick people out of the crowd – Pauline the soap mummy is one of the stories they decide to follow. And 'follow' is the operative word, here – when Paul sends her away to change into ordinary clothes, Pauline races around trying to find someone who'll lend her their clothes. One of the other auditionees agrees, and they race off to the nearest ladies' loo – and they're down to their bras before they realize a camera crew has come in after them. While her new best friend retires to a cubicle to get changed, Pauline's seemingly happy to wander around in her underwear for the camera. It makes for good TV, and Pauline is heavily featured in the first episode. When she gets the callback for the next day, she runs out of the hall, shouting to the panel that she loves them.

At Glasgow, there are a lot of men in kilts who decide to flash their backsides at the judges. So many, in fact, that one man gets through by promising not to.

Other people juggle eggs or eat fire. One woman flashes her breasts which have 'Pick Me Nigel' on them in felt tip, prompting Paul to suggest she's in the wrong show – an assessment Bill heartily concurs with.

Some of the shock tactics cross the line into the dangerous or irresponsible. One woman, Anne, goes up onto stage behind the panel, and tells them there's a fire alarm. The panel start the evacuation of the hall... only to learn it was one of the auditionees, trying to make a memorable

> **YVON GRACE, panellist**
>
> 'The process is fifteen seconds, you've only got that. Don't waste it. The people that wouldn't take no for an answer are not going to survive on a soap five seconds, let alone fifteen.'

impression. The judges remember her – but she's escorted from the building.

A moment later, someone's pointing a gun at Bill, and barking, 'Give me this part, or I'll fire!' This isn't the first time someone's pulled out a gun this morning, however.... Bill stares back at the latest gunman, completely unruffled. 'One more person points a gun at me, and I'll be so bored I'll effing want them to shoot me. No, thank you.'

Craig Henderson's is perhaps the most inventive way of getting the judges intrigued – he hands them a box with a photo and a phone number, and asks them to call if they are interested. They are and they do.

The vast majority of the hopefuls just do their best. Jon Miller's experience was perhaps typical:

'My name's Jon, and I'm a web designer by day but I'd much rather be a famous actor, so I made sure to make a date in my diary the moment the *Soapstars* auditions were announced. I didn't really think I'd stand much of a chance – I doubt I'm the world's greatest actor and at twenty-three I was probably too old for what they were looking for – but I want to be famous more than anything and I'm the sort of person that will grab at any straw no matter how unlikely. I thought that if you don't try, if you don't give it a go, then you won't ever know for sure that you wouldn't have been chosen. Besides, it would be televised – even if you're rubbish there's always a chance you could end up on the box, as *Popstars* proved!

'So I got up early on the day the London round of the *Soapstars* auditions were being held and arrived at the venue at about 8.30am, expecting to be the first in line. How wrong I was! There were already several hundred people in front of me. Still, the several hours of queuing gave plenty of time to chat with the other auditionees and work out just how we were going to try to impress the judges.

'The mix of people trying out was quite diverse. People from all ages, races and backgrounds were there, although considering a whole family was being auditioned most of the auditionees did seem under twenty-five, so maybe some of the adults were put off spending three hours in a queue of gregarious screaming kids! Discussion mostly consisted of trying to predict what the judges would be looking for, along with the presenter whipping everyone up to shout cries of "Pick me, Paul!" to the cameras and endless rounds of waving to the press.

'Once we were given our release forms to sign, along with details of the audition process, the work really began as everyone began thinking what to do with their fifteen seconds. Everyone felt it was too little time to be given a chance to shine, but I suppose it was the best way to guarantee that those chosen would be able to work under pressure.

'Eventually I got towards the front of the queue. In order to save time and get through auditionees quicker, me and about fifty others were siphoned off to an outdoor terrace where rather than going inside the building to be auditioned by a panel of judges we would be auditioned outdoors by just one judge, a lady named Yvon, who seemed to take a leaf out of Anne Robinson's book, both in appearance and manner.

'After waiting for several hours on the day of the auditions I finally neared the front of the queue and as I watched the people in front of me being dismissed one after the other it became clear how cut-throat this process was going to be.

'Still, I steeled myself for the moment when my fifteen seconds finally arrived and went forth unto the breach. I made the mistake of trying too hard to memorize the little script I'd written for myself while in the queue and while my audition started well I forgot my lines and stumbled trying to remember what to say, resulting in a "Thanks but no thanks" from Yvon. Oh well, I tried. I felt a bit embarrassed, as if I'd made a fool of myself by not being very good.

'Around me, some people were laughing at their failures; others were not taking things quite as well, but at the end of the day I couldn't be too upset as it was my own fault I didn't make it, and judging from the horror stories that followed as people picked themselves up from Yvon's cutting remarks, neither did most of the other people auditioning. One or two did slip through however, even though the rest of us had to go home.

'The whole process was great fun, even though I didn't make it past the first stage, but at least I can say a played a part, however small, in the whole *Soapstars* phenomenon.'

Three months later, Jon gets to see himself on television… in a crowd scene at the top of one of the early shows.

Yvon's got no qualms about rejecting people. 'I don't find it difficult to reject people that haven't got the talent or don't believe, or I personally don't believe, they can do it. If I absolutely believe that someone can do it, I'm with them, one hundred and fifty per cent,' she insists. 'And then it's hard to say goodbye, if I have to let them go. But if they haven't got it, there's no point in me investing anything and I just would say no. It's better for them in the long run.'

The groups are pretty evenly balanced between men and women – though there tend to be slightly more women. There are far, far more teens than adults. They sit, sometimes with the friend or family member they've brought in for moral support. Actors can be a superstitious lot – the vagaries of casting decisions don't encourage a rational view of how the world works. Now that the hopefuls are in the hall, everything seems to take on significance; mysterious things are happening. Everyone tries to second-guess what's going on, what the panel are looking for. Have the judges been out, secretly 'spotting' people with potential in the queue? If Sharon's pointing her roving camera at them, does that mean they've been earmarked as having potential? It seems to give those auditionees the encouragement that they've passed some secret test. Mostly, they watch the judges, try to read the runes. Bill's shaking his head. Paul's smiling. Yvon's looking at the woman on the stage at the moment, and whispers something to Paul. Paul chuckles and writes something down. The hopefuls take this as a good omen.

There are no runes to read. At this stage in the process, there's no hidden agenda, it's a simple exercise to divide those who have potential from those that don't. In this case, Yvon has just told Paul she likes the blue dress the woman is wearing. At the Glasgow audition, she stops one of the

> ### JON MILLER, auditionee L592, on Yvon
>
> 'This judge wasn't showing any mercy, and we joked that if *Popstars* had Nasty Nigel, *Soapstars* would have Evil Yvon.'

hopefuls as she is leaving the stage to ask where she bought her top. The judges take their responsibilities seriously, but in a lot of cases it's clear from the first couple of lines what the decision will be. For the sake of decency, even in the hopeless cases, they wait a little while before they confer and Paul calls out, 'That's all we need from you', but equally, they don't want to waste any more time than they have to. People get a fair shot, and the judges are allowing for a lack of experience and for nerves. But the winners will have to be up to scratch in eight weeks, no excuses.

The hopefuls mostly keep a respectful silence, although the occasional whisper of 'he's good' or 'her bum's *huge*' can be heard. People sit quietly and attentively. At some of the venues, the temperature is a little wilting, and it's often difficult to hear the performances, but people's attention doesn't wander. Rarely, there's a little round of applause – although, oddly perhaps, the audience never go for the same people as the judges.

the 'look'

Whatever else the fifteen-second audition might be, it's certainly an efficient way to reduce the numbers – typically, only something like one in a hundred people makes it to the next stage.

Over the next few weeks, one of the things the hopefuls will say – usually after having just been turned down – is that the judges 'know what they are looking for'. 'I'm blonde, and I've heard they're not looking for a blonde,' asserts one, apparently not noticing the large number of blondes who have already got through. A more general sentiment is that 'They've got a "look" in mind, and if your face doesn't fit, you don't make it'. They're right, in a way, but the hopefuls tend to think that it's a very narrow definition – that the judges have an exact person in mind, and are just waiting for them to walk up onto the stage.

The family, of course, have been drawn up with the casting process in mind – both parents were married before, they could have adopted a child, or come from different parts of the country. While the final family will have to work as a unit, they don't have to look alike, have the same body type or hair colour; they don't even have to come from the same ethnic group, or have the same accent. The judges have a free hand to pick who they think are the most talented people – they don't have a firm picture in their head for any of the parts.

So, the judges admit there's a 'look', but it's not quite as simple as it sounds. As Bill says: 'When I say "the look", it doesn't have to be someone that looks incredibly beautiful, although being honest I suspect somebody who looks incredibly wonderful you're going to put through just to see if they can do something as well, 'cos they're always useful....

'The joy of Lisa Riley when she came in the show was she was completely different.... She was virtually an extra, she had very little in the first episode but there was this like huge personality, very big girl and I immediately thought, "Yeah, I can do something with that." I remember her getting back in to the police van and then fighting her way out again, which was like a very small stage direction but

BILL LYONS, panellist

'One of my pet hates is when I flick through the channels and everybody looks the same. I think somebody that looks different stands a good chance.'

when you saw her do it, you thought you could do something with that because she was just a major personality. So personality is obviously important. And sometimes a personality can come through very quickly.'

Paul insists that there's a great deal of flexibility in the brief: 'If they're twenty-three, or twenty four, and they look younger, then that's fine. But at the end of the day, I've been chatting to the other two judges and we've decided that talent will out. We are really gonna push for that. So that if we have to change the brief a little bit then so be it.'

So what are the judges looking for? Bill Lyons: 'For me, it's the liveliness really. It's something going on behind the eyes. The thing that doesn't appeal to me is someone that tells you, "I'm what you're looking for because I am." Forget it. I mean, I'd rather somebody showed me. If they did something with a fairly instant impact and it's about a liveliness in the eyes, which is hard to describe but you know that there's something going on in there. And once you see that, it gives you such a lot of potential, 'cos you can do various things with them. But it's that dead look that really turns me off.

'If you look at the soap stars that I've worked with, and I've worked with a lot over the years, I think the qualities that you really admire in them are not always shown in the big scenes.... We have stars but there are going to be moments when everybody is not playing a major part in

'I'm looking for somebody who is natural, who totally under-stands and believes in themselves, who has a self-confidence, who is intelligent, who can interpret a script, learn it and repeat it and believe it. That's the person that would make a good soap actor.'

that scene or in that episode and they're keeping the character together.

'There are people who you always watch, even if they've only got tiny things to do. To go back to Leslie Grantham and Anita Dobson [Den and Angie in *EastEnders*]. One of the interesting things is that Anita behind the bar was often the most interesting thing in the scene in which she only had two lines, because she's still working, there's still that personality that comes across all the time. And she has an energy again, there's an energy and an enthusiasm that goes through. People don't realize how technically adept some actors are working in soap compared with others.'

Yvon's prepared to go a little further: 'I don't, hand on heart, think that the person who would make a good soap star would necessarily be somebody that has had loads of acting experience – and I'm probably going to get shot down in flames for saying that, but I really believe it. We're just talking about soap here, not Shakespeare or anything else – I, personally, am looking for naturalism.

'A good soap actor is also somebody who will work in a team and likes to work in a team, because that's soap. You basically become a member of a big telly family. And so, you know, there is a dynamic within the family, obviously, on a soap. Love/hate and all that going on. But it's essential to work as a team and not be an island.'

And what's a complete no-no? After a few open auditions, Yvon's now in a position to say: 'Having done it a few times, I could honestly say that if anybody touches me, or attempts to touch me, never mind what they're saying, they're just off. No way.

'The other thing I really can't stand is people coming on being really aggressive because they've waited outside for a while. Well, that isn't my fault. And they're standing there pointing at you, which is really, really horrible, because you've got nowhere to go, you can't move. And they get angry with you, personally, as if I've been going, "Can you make sure they stay out there for two and half hours?" So they've wasted fifteen seconds being annoyed at me for something I had nothing to do with anyway. So of course I'm not going to go, "Oh, yes please, I like you a lot."

'Bill's the one that hates the poems. I actually quite liked some of the poems on the quiet, I was going, "That's quite good, that." But Bill's like, "No", so, you know, we're the three musketeers, all for one, one for all and all that, so that was fine, poems were a no-go area. The shouting I can't stand. You know – that phrase, "I can't believe you're doing this to me." How many times have we heard that? The other one was the pregnancy thing. Me and Bill would sometimes say, "Can someone just be happy about the pregnancy?" As opposed to crying immediately that you're pregnant.

Yvon also recalls one woman in the Birmingham audition who read from a script she'd written herself. But with her head down, and a poor voice, she came across as boring and was soon rejected.... 'Anyway, I met her in the toilet afterwards, by accident, and she basically wouldn't let me out the door until I explained exactly why I said no to her.

YVON GRACE, panellist

'One person asked me if he could smoke! What, did I want to watch him smoke a cigarette for fifteen seconds?'

Now, if she's watching this, that was really not a useful thing to do, thanks very much. Don't ever do that to anybody else again.'

Paul's got his own pet hate: 'One thing that I hate is chewing gum as well, because it's just such a mark of disrespect. I think that it looks awful, you play back the camera, particularly if it's a film or a television commercial [and] it looks like they're chewing the cud, you know it looks absolutely awful and it's common. And I don't like anything common.'

the scene

The judges very quickly whittle down the numbers on Day Two, with only a few hundred getting through to the second stage, being sent away overnight to learn a scene from *Emmerdale*. Paul: 'When we were working with the scripts, some of them worked better for me than others. The Bob and Viv scene I found particularly difficult to deal with because it was comedy and most people didn't know how to play that kind of comedy. And in fairness to the people that were auditioning for it, I don't think they understood the scene....

'But some of the other scripts did work well. Kathy and Andy I liked. The Marlon and Tricia one worried me a little bit, when he had to keep smelling her hair. I didn't like that either but all in all there were scenes that were taken out. I wasn't expecting to see polished, finished performances at any point and I'm still not. The talent is gonna be raw and some people made something out of it and some people didn't. And I was OK about that.'

At this stage, the panellists are keen to see people demonstrating good technique, and the hopefuls have had a day to learn the script, so they are expected to know it. But they aren't too worried about the odd dropped line – they see qualities in a couple of people who fluff lines, Sarah Smart and Jason Hain, which means they get through to the semis, although they'll have a lot to prove next time around.

improvisation

If they satisfy the judges, the hopefuls go through to stage three, where they have to work together in groups of three to improvise a scene. Already the numbers are down to almost manageable levels – of the 5,000, only 129 make it to stage three.

Yvon's happy. 'I was pleased when Tim said they were going to do impro, because I was an actress, as well as a drama producer, and I always think it's very, very important to be able to see that the actor that you're going to get has got that flexibility. That they can understand what they're saying and actually change it within seconds, if called upon. And that's what impro does. It makes you stay in the moment, and think ahead the whole time, while concentrating on what you're saying. And that's a very brilliant skill that most soap actors have. So I think there is a connection really between the impro and soap.'

Bill's not convinced the improvisations themselves are much use, but concedes they do have value: 'We're not in a perfect world. I mean, a soap is so far from a perfect world it's not true. People have personal problems and all sorts of things, so things have to be changed. And so the, the ability to think on your feet is useful because you'll find yourself doing scenes you weren't expecting to be doing, scenes that were originally written for someone else and have to be altered so that they can tell the story using other characters....

'... the one thing I get out of improvisation is how quickly somebody can think on their feet. I'd sooner just give them another scene and say, "Get this together as quickly as you can," because that's more like what they're going to do.'

One hopeful, Johnny Kinch, decides his improvisation will be autobiographical – about the day he decided to draw a line under his troubles and rebuild his life. It's a decision that puts the backs up of the fellow hopefuls in the scene, because it relegates them to almost bit parts. But it impresses the judges, and Johnny gets through.

the camera test

It's stage four already on the last day of the auditions.

Stage four involves the hopefuls going up one at a time, sitting in front of the judges and having a brief chat. It's a way of seeing a bit more of them at ease, to let their personalities come to the forefront. But the main purpose is far more prosaic – it's a screen test. The judges watch their monitors, rather than looking directly at the actors. Bill explains why: 'The camera test is important because it's about age range. It's not what you are, it's what you look like. I know that from personal experience, because when

BILL LYONS, panellist

'People think, "Oh, but I gave a great performance, why am I not in the show?" Well, if you don't look like somebody that could be part of that family, there's no real point.'

I was still acting, when I was twenty-seven I was still playing teenagers, which was one of the things that drove me to write instead of act – I was really fed up with playing kids in leather jackets that beat up old ladies when I was twenty-seven and was actually a father of two....

'It's tough, particularly tough for somebody that has given a good performance but then you look at them and you think, "They don't look old enough to be parent and they look too old to be a teenager." And the problem with that is, we talked about flexibility, but you're saying something about a character. Supposing somebody is twenty-two [and they] move to a village. Well, it says something about the character if you move with your parents or a parent at twenty-two to a village. It says something immediately about the character which is with you for the whole time you're in the show.... So you've said something about the character, and it's not something that you can ignore.'

Performances and faces can be transformed by television. People look fatter (it's an actor's adage that the 'camera adds ten pounds'), their faces can change shape – beautiful people can become odd looking, while people you wouldn't look at twice in the street can look stunning. It's a weird process and no one's sure how it works. Some technical people will talk about the dimensions of the TV screen itself; others will say that as most people on TV are slim, an average-sized person will look fat.

Yvon agrees: 'Yeah, it's interesting that, because even a good-looking person very often can look plainer on camera than they do in the flesh. And – don't ask me why, it's probably something to do with science and technology – but that is absolutely a truism. Very often you'll meet people that have got very good bone structure – they're going to look good on camera. A very pretty girl with a round face, round features, might just look bland on camera.'

The judges discuss their choices – who's good enough to go to the semi-final. As a rough estimate, they want less than a hundred to get through, ideally about seventy-five. On the whole, it's pretty obvious who's got what it takes. There are a few that split opinion – a few of the hopefuls, like Ashra Price and Victoria Tonge, are good actors, but look too old to play the daughter, too young to play the mum. Yvon's got the knife out for Ashra:

YVON: *She's in-between age groups.*

PAUL: *She's in for me.*

BILL: *Looking at that screen –*

YVON: *I don't think she looks old enough to be the mum.*

BILL: *Not at all, she's young –*

PAUL: *She's young enough to be the daughter.*

YVON: *I don't think she looks young enough to be the daughter. She's a no for me. She failed the screen test.*

PAUL: *She didn't for me.*

BILL: *Funnily enough, she didn't for me, and I'm a swine.*

YVON: *She looks... twenty-... eight. I'm not convinced at all.*

PAUL: *Not too old for me.*

BILL: *Nor me.*

YVON: *What's that then? Yes or no?*

PAUL: *Yes.*

BILL: *Yes.*

YVON: *She looks too old. She can't carry off twenty-one on camera, in my view.*

BILL: *OK. I beg to differ, because I think she probably can.*

PAUL: *Yeah.*

YVON: *OK... I'm going home.*

Was it really all up to the judges, or did the *Soapstars* producer Tim Miller put pressure on them to get 'characters' into the show? 'As for influencing the process, yes I tried,' he admits. 'I wanted the judges to help us out with certain stories. I didn't feel it would do any harm to the individuals concerned because it would simply give them more exposure, which would undoubtedly help them if they wanted to be actors. But the panel wouldn't play ball.

'We had a bit of a showdown in Birmingham after which I realized that I would not be able to influence any of their decisions. They had rejected Elizabeth Bowden on the grounds that she looked too old. I wanted her to be kept in because she had made Yvon cry when she acted out her scene (and was therefore a good story). I also wanted her in because she looked much younger than people who had

BILL LYONS, panellist

'If you had a superstar and you put them on the screen, you wouldn't necessarily recognize them within fifteen seconds. So you've just got to go on gut instinct.'

been let through in Sheffield. The panel had got tighter to the brief. That's fine. As time went on, this was only natural. But my concern was that the Sheffield and Birmingham auditions would be cut together in the same programme and the panel might therefore look inconsistent.'

By the end of the open auditions, the judges have seen 4,900 people and picked sixty-four to go through to the semi-finals in London at the beginning of August. It's fewer than they were expecting, but that's no great concern. However, a genuine problem has become apparent – they expected a lot more youngsters to turn up to the open auditions than adults, but it had been hoped that what the adults lacked in quantity, they'd make up for in quality. That hasn't proved to be the case. Looking at the lists, it's clear they are particularly short of dads. Reviewing their options, the judges see they've got some promising candidates, particularly in Johnny Kinch and a candidate from the Glasgow auditions, Brian McDevitt. They only need one winner, but at this stage they want flexibility. If they're limited by their choice of parents, they could end up seriously limiting their options with the other casting. They don't want to have to fit the casting of the others around the casting of the dad, at least not at this stage.

Bill Lyons is sure of one reason why they've not had many adults come forward – 'If you're a forty-year-old actor who's not had any work, it's almost certainly because you're no good. Or you've spent fifteen years in prison. You ask them what they've done before, and they say, "A lot of work on the stage"; they don't tell you they were sweeping it.' Can you believe that the press release for *Soapstars* describes Bill as a 'curmudgeon'? He goes on to admit that a lot of actresses give up their profession in their twenties to raise a family, but, perhaps sensing people might think he's gone soft, qualifies that with the comment 'but that's not always a loss to the industry'.

At the suggestion of Keith Richardson, an extra open audition is quickly arranged, and advertised in *The Stage* and in the press. It will take place only a week before the semi-finals....

final open audition

CHAPTER THREE

*Friday 27 July, 2001. A week to go before the
semi-finals and ten more adults are needed to
raise the number of 'mums' and 'dads'.
700 people are reduced to eight.*

This extra audition, like the larger London one, takes place
at the Rocket Complex, a venue at the University of North
London. Crash barriers are erected outside, and the crowds
of would-be soap stars arrive. There's a healthy turnout –
around seven hundred. There are a few people there when
the *Soapstars* crew arrives at six, but no evidence that
anyone's camped out overnight, as at the bigger auditions.

Once everything's been set up inside, production assis-
tants go back outside, walk down the queue, picking off the
people in the wrong age range, and warning them that
they're not what *Soapstars* is looking for this time out – this
audition is specifically for the parents of the new family. Most
people get the message – and many seem relieved. Being
turned down because your face doesn't fit, without being
given a fair chance to demonstrate your skills is, it seems, less
soul-destroying than giving it all you've got and still being
rejected. At least at this stage it's not personal. Besides, it's
another hot day, even by nine in the morning, and there are
better things to do than standing on a hot pavement for

several hours only to spend a minute or two inside before ending up back out on the pavement. A few gamely stay on, not taking the hint. One girl, auditioning for the part of the mother of two grown-up teenagers, gives her age as twenty-seven, and looks younger. Another claims to be forty-six, but is clearly much older. The three judges amuse themselves trying to guess her real age – the lowest estimate is seventy.

There are people here who wouldn't have dreamt of coming to the earlier auditions. Talking to the hopefuls here today, it's clear many of the actors in their thirties and forties didn't like the sound of the 'fifteen-second' stage, feeling that was the part of the process that was particularly demeaning for a professional actor. The adult audition skips straight to the reading of a scene, the second stage at the previous open auditions. Mark Jardine, one of those towards the back of the queue at Sheffield who decided not to stay very long, is one of the first to get through to the semis today. Most of the others here simply decided not to turn up to the bigger auditions in the first place.

The age restriction might be frustrating for actors who find themselves turned away at the door for being born in the wrong year, but the parts on offer are for the parents of teenaged children, after all. As it's adults being auditioned this time, there are far less 'eccentrics'. Just about all the men are wearing smart-casual clothes – shirt and slacks. There's more variety in what the women are wearing, and a couple are 'dressed to impress' in sequinned crop tops, but most opt for sensible summer dresses. The judges, who never seem to be happy about anything, are a bit worried that a lot of the people look a bit dull. One thing that's striking, even within the preferred age range of 'about thirty-five to about fifty', is just how much variation there is.

Men and women of all shapes, sizes and colours have turned up.

While no two hopefuls look the same, they do have a lot of other things in common. As Keith Richardson predicted, a lot of people here are actors already. Julie Woodman is typical of the people who've come here after seeing the advert in *The Stage*. She's recently completed an HND in Performing Arts, and she's done some local theatre work, she's been an extra on TV, and played the lead role in a ten-minute short that Channel Four are showing later in the year. Her son, Nick, has come along to support her. He looks composed, at home, and it soon becomes clear why – he's studying at the acclaimed Sylvia Young drama school. One of the past graduates is Sheree Murphy, who plays Tricia in *Emmerdale*, and her classmates there included Denise Van Outen, Emma Bunton, Keeley Hawes, Samantha Janus and Martine McCutcheon. Another graduate, although not from the same year, was *Soapstars* judge Paul de Freitas. As well as acting and other performance skills, the school teaches audition technique and relaxation exercises – so, ironically, out of the hundreds of people in the queue, Nick could well be the person best-quali-fied to cope with what's ahead.

The hopefuls are handed one of a number of three- or four-page scenes from *Emmerdale*. There's no such thing as a 'generic' scene, but these show typical situations from a soap opera – Sean confesses an affair to Angie; Marlon and Tricia disagree about the future of their relationship; Lisa tells Cynthia about discovering she was pregnant in her forties; and, printed here, Paddy proposes to Mandy:

[Paddy has left the Vets' Ball to find his ex-girlfriend Mandy]

PADDY: *Mandy? You were there tonight weren't you? I found this.*

[Holds Mandy's necklace]

MANDY: *It was a stupid idea. I should never have come.*

PADDY: *Why didn't you come and talk to me?*

MANDY: *Because you were with Bernice enjoying yourself. I didn't want to spoil things for you.*

PADDY: *You daft thing. I had a miserable time. I've had a miserable time since we split up.*

MANDY: *So have I.*

PADDY: *And I'm fed up of pretending that I'm all right without you and that I'm over losing you because I'm not.*

MANDY: *Me neither.*

PADDY: *I was thinking tonight when I was dancing with Bernice. I was thinking that the only woman that I want to dance with the only woman in the whole wide world was you.*

MANDY: *Do you really mean that?*

PADDY: *Will you dance with me now?*

MANDY: *There's no music.*

PADDY: *I can hear music.*

MANDY: *I can hear music too.*

[They dance]

PADDY: *Mandy?*

MANDY: *What?*

PADDY: *Marry me.*

The lack of punctuation is deliberate – to act a scene out, an actor has to understand it. And if they understand it, they can put their own pauses and emphases in. All the scenes require the actors to demonstrate a variety of emotions, they all balance a disagreement of some kind with a more gentle, often humorous, undertone. None of the scenes is a doddle to play; all have a couple of potential pitfalls. But all four scenes are real scenes from *Emmerdale.* The Paddy and Mandy scene was originally the last scene of the 2,500th episode, a memorable hour-long special (written by Chris Thompson and broadcast in March 1999), that reinterpreted the *Cinderella* story with Mandy as Cinders and Bernice and Tricia as the ugly sisters who wouldn't let her go to the annual Vets' Ball. This is the sort of material the winners will have to perform – and those winners will be starting work on the show in eight weeks. The audition is a fair test.

The hopefuls are paired off, and given about an hour to rehearse with their new partner. Most do so inside, in the shade of the Rocket Complex bar.

One 'Marlon and Tricia' pair are Andy White and Maria Sophia Andreas. Andy's a management consultant from the Midlands; Maria Sophia lives in Islington, and works with people who have psychiatric problems. Andy's mainly here to support his sister, but is enjoying a day off. Maria Sophia's recently joined an amateur dramatic group, and has done some work as an extra. She's been bitten by the acting bug, and isn't sure how to take it any further. They'd not even met each other in the queue before they were paired off, and now find themselves rehearsing a scene in which Andy objects to his girlfriend Maria Sophia's plan to marry a gay friend who needs a visa. So, is Maria Sophia anything like Andy's real wife? Is Andy Maria Sophia's type? Both get a fit of the giggles when they're asked, and pretend to be scandalized.

They start practising their scene – it's only about two minutes long, so an hour ought to be plenty of time to work through any problems. They're not expected to learn the lines (although some will, or will hardly refer to their script). At this stage the judges will be looking for an understanding of the part, evidence of interpretation – to see people acting, in other words, not just reading. Andy and Maria Sophia both seem relaxed; Andy makes jokes and they chat between 'takes'. Both see today as an opportunity to do something new. Andy chuckles that he's sure his staff could run his office if he was to land the part, but doubts they'll have to. Maria Sophia is realistic about her chances, but wants to develop a career as an actress, and sees this as experience that will hold her in good stead later – and today could be her big break.

The hopefuls are divided into groups of a couple of dozen. When it's their time, the first group is led up a lurid green stairwell to the main hall. The room could be the venue for a concert, and could seat 300. Today, all the action is at the far end. The hopefuls are led to one side of the room. As they take their seats, they look up at the impressive curved ceiling and note that it's seen better days. There's a simple set-up on stage – the three judges sit behind a table, Paul in the middle. The centre of the stage is where the performances take place, under the glare of lighting rigs. A cameraman with a hefty camera perched on his shoulder circles the performers. A sound man pushes his boom mike towards them.

It's a hot day as it is, but onstage it's withering. More than one person will compare the combination of bright lights, oppressive temperatures and five people staring at their every move to some kind of torture. The combination of the hottest day of the year and the fact the hopefuls are older than those from the initial auditions means that there isn't the exuberance of the larger auditions. Sharon Walker, patrolling the room with her hand-held camera, is worried she won't get enough material. In the event, this audition is mentioned in the programme, but no footage from it is shown.

The judges take it in turns to give a short pep talk to the groups as they come in, explaining the basics. The auditionees aren't to cross the line marked out in black tape on the stage, they're to look at the panel, not the cameras, and if it's not their turn, they're to keep quiet when a performance is underway.

A few basic common errors are repeated. A fair few, perhaps used to stage work, are projecting their voices to the back of the hall. Others aren't sure what to do with their hands, and settle for grand gestures. A worrying number seem to be reading the lines, rather than acting them – missing the emotion, putting the emphasis on the wrong words, even misreading what's on the page in front of them. One of the Angies reads the phrase 'Christmas presents' and decides the second word is a verb. One line in particular is giving the 'Marlons' trouble –

'It's just that old story, isn't it? Boy meets girl, boy falls in love with girl, girl marries gay man. No problem there, no problem at all.' *Emmerdale* viewers will recognize Marlon's trademark sarcasm, which is normally brought to manic life by Mark Charnock. Not many of the hopefuls get the full value from the line – a number stumble over it, a couple don't seem to spot that Marlon's being ironic. It's not an easy line to judge, it needs a mix of comic timing and the momentum of a snarling rant.

Yvon: 'It might be a problem, in that people might overdo it, make it a more camp scene. And in that sense we won't be able to judge really what that person's ability really is. Because there is an awful lot of campery in that scene. So as far as I'm concerned, no, it's not a very good one. But I have seen it done properly on the actual show – I don't know the actor's name that plays Marlon, but he did it very well.'

In the front row, four hopefuls sit, waiting for their turns. A95 is Harriet James, A110 is Roger Wentworth, and they'll be Angie and Sean. A97 is Debra Fougere and A123 is Terry Turnbill, they've got the Mandy and Paddy script. Anyone knowing *Emmerdale* would find the thought of a short Paddy and a tall, slim Mandy a little incongruous. None of the four watches *Emmerdale*, though, so that's not something that they'll think about.

They sit patiently. Harriet stretches, does some breathing exercises, gives Roger a quick neckrub. She confirms she studied drama. Debra has also just finished a two-year course. Harriet jokes about having just come in from Hollywood – then admits she's from Finsbury Park, two stops from here on the Piccadilly Line. Debra's from Richmond. Terry's from Essex. Roger's come from Peterborough. They've all been to auditions before, which have led to stage work and some non-speaking roles on TV.

Roger's done a couple of speaking parts. He seems the most confident of the four. Debra holds her hand out, and it's shaking a little. Harriet is keeping herself calm. Terry's staying quiet.

Harriet and Roger go up first. The judges ask them to start from the top of page two – page one has a lot of Sean, and not very much for Angie to do. This puts Harriet off her stride a little, but she rallies. They complete their scene. Unlike the previous auditions, the panel don't announce their verdicts until they've seen the whole group. So, Paul thanks them, and Roger and Harriet head back to their seats. Roger thinks he did his best; Harriet is sure she could have done better. Debra and Terry go next. The judges don't quite let them get to the end of their scene, so they don't have to dance with each other. They both seem glad it's over.

The announcement of who, if anyone, is going through to the semi-finals waits until everyone in the group has had their turn. The four people in the front row wait, a little nervously. Once everyone's been seen, a couple of the people are given another scene to try. The judges aren't sure about a couple of them, and want to see them again, playing a different part, or playing opposite another actor. Roger's number is called out... but it's a mistake. They want A101, not A110. Roger stands up, then realizes the mistake and sits down. He's smiling about it before he's back down in the chair.

Once the whole group has been seen, the judges come to the front and announce their decision. It traditional to say that there was a lot of competition, that it was a difficult choice. In some cases it genuinely has been. One person from the twenty-six goes through, a woman called Barbara,

TIM MILLER, *Soapstars* producer

'Obviously we knew what the panel were thinking so we had inside knowledge, but it was hard because even the panel changed their minds about people. It was very hard to second guess which stories would last.'

one of the ones they asked to see again. The group of four commiserate with each other, then make their way out of the hall, with everyone else. They're all naturally disappointed, particularly Roger, who looked to have come close. All four are philosophical – this is good experience; at least they found out quickly; there's nothing wrong with them, it's just that their faces didn't fit…. Terry notes wryly that all the platitudes are being wheeled out, and they smile. On their way down, they meet the next group on the way up.

Between groups, the judges take a quick break. Bill and Yvon light up cigarettes; Paul's already on his tiny red mobile phone. How do they think it's going? 'The Paddy and Mandy scene as done by *Emmerdale* was superb, it was brilliant,' Paul gushes. 'And so I was expecting more from that scene than people gave, actually, but it was a very well-written scene. Very often you would find somebody – frustratingly it was never Paddy and Mandy at the same time – who made sense of that scene and made it a wonderful thing…. But that was a useful scene to use, because it was emotive. It was emotional and it had a build to it. It started off small and got bigger.'

Tim and the *Soapstars* team are milling around Barbara, conducting a quick to-camera interview, recording her initial reactions. They discover that Barbara isn't an actress, but she's a soap addict – she's instinctively picked up the sort of acting style the judges are looking for. Bill's had a quick chat with her, and he's impressed: 'For me, it validates this whole process if we can discover people like Barbara.' The judges don't know beforehand what acting experience or how much formal training the hopefuls have had – they are basing their decision entirely on what they see in the audition itself, and not making allowances for inexperience.

Barbara is, of course, surprised and delighted to get a place in the semi-finals, particularly with so few people getting through. With her short interview recorded, she's led out to a corridor to check her details, and a Polaroid photo is taken and stapled to her form, for future reference. After that, Denzil takes a few proper publicity photos. Then she's given information about the semi-finals, a week today, and heads off home, smiling, but looking a little dazed.

By then, the next group is already halfway done. They aren't showing much promise – the judges can tell that some of them won't pass muster before they've even made it to the stage, and the hopefuls don't do anything that persuades them that they are unfairly making snap judgements. There are thirty people in the group, so that means there'll be fifteen performances of a two-minute scene, plus time getting to and from the stage, and setting-up time. The judges whisk through, giving people a fair chance to overcome initial nerves, and always leaving a decent interval before gently telling them, 'That's all we need from you.' But even so, the whole group is seen in seventeen minutes flat, and it's the first group of the day where no one showed enough promise to make it to the semis.

There's a short break and the judges huddle, shaking their heads. 'There was a range in that group,' Bill growls, 'some were crap, and some were deeply crap.' Paul's on his phone, but nods his agreement. Yvon's more positive – 'We could get a whole cast out of that group – if we were casting for a series called *Menopause City*'.

A new phenomenon is becoming obvious – a couple of those hopefuls had already been in, earlier in the morning. It's not too difficult to find discarded badges downstairs, and some people have taken one and doubled back, deciding to give it another shot. They must be gambling that the judges see so many people they won't remember them. Yvon reckons that would probably be fair, and can't be sure exactly how many are trying it on – but there are three or four who don't so much stand out, as look like *Fast Show* characters. The man with the spiky hair, the man in the *Prisoner* blazer, the girl in the spangly white crop top. Yvon picks a fight with one of them on stage –

– *'I've seen you before.'*

– *'Nah, love, you haven't.'*

– *'You were here this morning. I've seen you before.'*

– *'I've been in* London's Burning. *You've seen me in that.'*

Needless to say, none of them has discovered what it takes to get through to the next round in the hour since they were first rejected. When someone spots a 'repeat', one of the PAs is sent over to give a gentle warning that they've been rumbled. At that point, most take the hint and go, but a couple of them stay on to be rejected again. One man tries three times before getting the message. Bill notes that 'he was crap… three times'.

Andy White and Maria Sophia Andreas are in the next group. They take their places in the hall, waiting to be called. They say they aren't nervous, and Andy doesn't look it. Maria Sophia's a little more on edge – she's keen to make a good impression. They sit, and do what everyone else in the room is doing – try to read the runes that aren't there; watch the couples who go up before them, looking for tips; whisper snap judgements. Andy's suddenly worried his face won't fit. He knows they've already completed the audition for the children, and so they'll have specific types in mind to match up with who's already been chosen. What if they don't look like him? He wants to tell the judges that although he's of average height, he's got sons who are 6'2", 6'4", even one who's 6'8".

One woman, in a red dress, is leaving the stage when Paul asks her to turn back to check her badge number. Andy and Maria Sophia agree that this has to mean she's caught their eye.

It's Andy and Maria Sophia's turn. They smile at each other, and make their way to the stage. The studio lights glare, but aren't actually that hot. It's stifling enough without them, though. Andy and Maria Sophia take their place on the stage, carefully not crossing their mark on the stage. The cameraman works his way around them, the sound man keeps the microphone boom just out of shot. The camera lens is barely inches away from their faces. The judges watch them intently, nodding from time to time. This is the first time Andy's been on a stage since a school play. Rather than being nervous, both agree later that they got a buzz from being on the stage, that they enjoyed themselves. And it shows: both he and Maria Sophia do well – Andy delivers the difficult 'girl meets gay man' line with gusto, earning a nod or two from the judges. Andy and Maria gel as a couple, and they are clearly well prepared.

They get all the way through their two minutes without the judges calling time, and the 'Thank you' Paul gives them seems genuine enough.

The two hopefuls sit back down, both pleased they've done their best. They speculate about how they've done – they were concentrating on acting, not on the judges, but they are feeling optimistic. Maria Sophia agrees with Andy that she was expecting to be nervous, but says when she got up onto the stage, that evaporated and it was exhilarating. Only about half the group have had their turn, so they're going to have to wait ten or fifteen minutes for the verdict. They take comfort in the next couple – surely they weren't as bad as *that?* Downstairs, both were fairly nonchalant about their chances – now they think they might have made it.

They've got another half an hour to wait. The judges finish the group, but want to check something. The three of them join Tim and Marnie at the monitor, and ask to see the recording of one of the hopefuls. Andy and Maria Sophia are on the left-hand side of the hall, and, like everyone else there, they can lean in and get a glimpse of the screen. They try to work out who the judges are watching. When they spot it's a blonde woman, Andy starts rehearsing what the judges will say, and Maria Sophia joins in – they'll all be told it was a tough choice, everyone did very well, but that only a few people made it. Neither now thinks they'll make the cut. The judges eventually break away from their monitors, shaking their heads. Yvon addresses the group. As predicted, Yvon thanks them for coming, but only the woman in the red dress has made it.

Andy isn't surprised, but is a little disappointed – he thought he'd done well. He's surprised how much he enjoyed himself, and would be surprised if this was the last acting he tried his hand at. He leaves the hall, joining his sister, who also didn't get through.

Maria Sophia is also disappointed, but is serious about pursuing a career and wants some feedback from the judges. They are clearly picking a very small number to go through – so how close did she get? With hundreds of people still to see, the judges don't have much time to spare, but Paul has a couple of encouraging words, and suggests she sends a CV, with a photograph, to the casting director at LWT. The station receive a lot of unsolicited CVs like that – but they also make a lot of programmes, and do keep the information on file. There's a chance a director might see the photo and cast Maria Sophia in a small role. It's not the big break Maria Sophia wanted, but it's good experience, and only stiffened her resolve to try again.

Yvon has seen one of the Rocket Complex's security guards, Terry, and jokes that they should get him to try out. Bill takes her seriously, and goes for a chat with him. Terry is charming, affable – and has absolutely no intention of auditioning. Bill tells him they're being serious – but Terry laughs that he's famous enough as it is. He's quite happy in the job he's got.

Dee Whitehead, the woman in the red dress who's through to the finals, is an ex-hairdresser from Nottingham, and has been a professional actress for a year. She's been an extra in a number of TV shows, such as *Peak Practice* and *Playing the Field*. She recently had a small speaking role in the new *Crossroads*, and can be seen right at the end of the film *Billy Elliot*. She has an agent, who tipped her off about this audition, but she's not earning a living from her acting – she's grateful for the support from her husband, Paul.

Before becoming an actress, Dee was a hairdresser for nearly thirty years, while also working in amateur dramatics and for a theatre co-operative. 'I'm a little bit dazed, to be honest with you. I can't believe I'm through, or that so few other people have got through.'

Unknown to the *Soapstars* production team, Dee's father died the day before the open audition. However, her mum wanted her to carry on rather than abandon her golden chance to become an actress. Dee didn't want it to affect the judges' decision – she wants to get through on the merits of her performance, she doesn't want allowances made, or to be the sympathy vote. She knows he'd be proud of her.

Dee wonders who to phone first – her husband, her mum... she settles for a friend who lives nearby. Before she can do that, she has her photo taken and Tim conducts a quick interview with her.

Yvon and Bill have caught up with another woman from the group – she wasn't right for this part, but both think she's a good actress. When they discover she's a cleaner, with no previous experience, they encourage her to keep trying, perhaps join an amateur dramatics group, and to try to get an agent. The woman leaves, smiling. Yvon hopes she realizes they were serious, and that she sticks with it – she was one of barely a handful of people to get that sort of encouragement, and the judges are not exactly generous with their praise.

There's one last group to get through – the one with the woman who says she's forty-six but whom the judges felt was nearer her seventies. The judges have a good laugh about that, and this last group of the day actually produces two semi-finalists.

It's 4.15pm, and the last of the hopefuls has left the building. Most of the *Soapstars* crew have been here since 6am. There were no quotas today, but they were hoping to find about ten people. In the event, they found eight, from about 700 hopefuls. Of the eight selected to go through to the semis, only three were men. While they only need one actor to be the father of the new family, that man will have to work well with the rest of the winners. Everyone's a little nervous that they've not got enough male contenders into the semis to have much of a choice. But, other than that, it's been a good day, and the judges are really keen on a number of the people they've picked.

making soapstars

Of course, the *Soapstars* production team also has its own deadlines to meet and challenges to face. Their task is to shape the footage into an exciting TV programme. To pick out whose stories are worth following, to earmark the most entertaining hopefuls. At this stage, they aren't too worried about spotting winners – they know who made it to the semi-finals, of course, and will follow some of those, but they've got no idea who the finalists will be, let alone the winners. Tim's not worried about that, and points out that *Popstars* went for weeks and weeks before there was even a glimpse of any of the eventual winners. The aim at this point is to make entertaining television, to find the interesting stories.

And the paradox is that the most entertaining *Soapstars* hopefuls in the early stages are the ones who stood no chance of getting through to the semis. Dressing eccentrically and behaving irrationally earned a swift 'No' from the

TIM MILLER, *Soapstars* producer

'As things progressed we started to pick people who we knew had gone a long way – particularly those in the final ten. We were cutting the second semi-final programme while the finals were taking place. And by the time we cut the finals we knew who our family was.'

judges – it was entirely the wrong tactic to impress a panel looking for acting talent and an appreciation of the requirements of soap opera. But it's one of the best tactics to get on these early *Soapstars* programmes.

The editors break up the footage into categories – each team has a slightly different label, but they all seem to break the contestants down into Loonies (the ones dressed and acting oddly), Optimists (the people convinced, often against all the evidence, that they have what it takes), Talent (the people with a chance) and Stories (people who've, for example, camped out overnight or come a long way).

With nearly 6,000 people to choose from, Tim Miller explains why they decided to follow who they did: 'We were looking for people who did something out of the ordinary – hence Craig Henderson and his box, Dean Abrahams sneaking past the queue in London. Then there were the childhood sweethearts, Will and Jude. Human interest stories or good characters were what we would follow. Sometimes we were lucky and these people progressed. Sometimes (Sue Sweeney) they were booted out faster than we would have hoped. We were actually quite lucky in that Dean, Craig, Jason and Johnny Kinch all progressed a long way.'

And with the open auditions done, things are about to get far more serious....

the long weekend

CHAPTER FOUR

Saturday 4 August to Monday 6 August, 2001.
The semi-finals: seventy-two are whittled down
to thirty-three, then twenty-five.

day one

From nearly 6,000 hopefuls, the judges have picked just
seventy-two people to make it through to the next round.
The semi-finals take place over a long weekend –
Saturday morning to Monday evening. One of the most
common sentiments expressed in that time will be that
people have done well to get this far. Some people are
amazed they're through to the semis. One woman,
Becky, was only at the Birmingham audition to report on
Soapstars for her radio station, Atlantic 252. She was
dared to enter the competition, and found herself called
back two days running. Now she's wondering if she'll
make it to the final.

The hopefuls are all staying at a good London hotel,
and most have started making friends with other semi-finalists. It's noticeable how well everyone is getting on – while
this is a competition, and most of the people here are
taking it very seriously, there's no bitterness, even towards
their direct rivals. Moreover, no one left here just wants to
be on TV to be famous; everyone's seeing it as an acting
challenge, a job application.

The first day of the semi-finals is to take place at the London Studios, the same place a number of LWT shows, not to mention GMTV, are filmed. As it's a Saturday, *SM:TV* is being broadcast, live from the next studio. Although very few of the *Soapstars* hopefuls notice, they are sharing a canteen with the latest boyband, and a couple of kids' TV celebrities. Outside the studios, there's a queue of teenage girls waiting to catch a glimpse of Ant and Dec and their guests. The *Soapstars* auditions will take place in Studio One, where *Blind Date* is recorded. Today it's bare, with just a large black curtain and a desk for the judges to sit behind.

The aim at this stage is to see how the hopefuls handle more serious, sustained acting challenges. They've been sent a couple of scenes to learn, one of which is a 'kissing scene'. The judges suspect their first task will be to weed out the people who were lucky to make it. There are no targets or quotas, but they'll have to lose about two-thirds of the people here. By Monday afternoon, they'll have whittled down the hopefuls to twenty-five finalists – ideally, five for each of the five parts on offer, but they've still got a lot more mums than dads, and plenty of kids (especially girls), so that might not be the exact ratio.

The hopefuls have all been given more scenes from *Emmerdale* to learn. It's immediately obvious that most, if not all, of the semi-finalists are serious contenders. The standard of the acting is far better than that in the regional heats; there are few fluffed lines and over-stagy perform-ances. The judges had advised people to watch soaps, to get a feel for the style of performance, and it's clear that a lot of people are pitching it right. At the same time, a couple of hopefuls are still quite stilted, or lose their place.

YVON GRACE, panellist

'It's no more Mr Nice Guy, we're going to be really ruthless. They've had the script for two weeks, so they should know it.'

While the hopefuls don't know what parts are on offer yet, they know the judges are looking to cast a family, and it's clear that most of the actors are suitable for roles as either a mum, a dad, a son or a daughter. Some, though, are 'in-betweeners'. Victoria Tonge is twenty-nine. The judges are impressed with her performance, but she's too old to play a teenager, and the judges aren't sure she'll be convincing as the mother of teenage kids. There are about a dozen people in the same position – slightly too old or slightly too young to be members of the family they've got in mind. On the stage, it wouldn't be a problem. On TV, it's more of an issue, but it's not insurmountable. A lot can be done with costume and make-up, and, most importantly, a good performance could persuade an audience. Victoria is sent to the make-up department, where Jo Frye will try to add a few years.

It is, of course, pretty unusual for a woman to try make herself look older using make-up – at least once she's reached the age that she can get into pubs. It is possible to age people by decades using elaborate latex make-up, sculpting wrinkles and lines. It happens a lot in films, but it's a process that takes many hours, and would be impractical in a soap. And it's not needed here – all Jo has to do is make a woman in her late twenties look like she's in her early thirties.

First, Jo darkens the area around Victoria's eyes, because that's a key cue people use when guessing someone's age.

Everything else is a matter of style, rather than changing the shape of the face. Victoria's hair has a trendy ruffled look. In the limited time she's got, Jo 'relaxes' it, flattening and combing it into a more conservative style. She also darkens Victoria's eyebrows. Older women's cheekbones tend to be sharper, so Jo emphasizes that. None of the make-up she uses is special TV make-up, it's all available off the shelf. Studio lights can be unforgiving, though, so Jo's using more than you'd use ordinarily, even if you were off to a club. Victoria's done a lot of theatre work, and it's nothing compared with the make-up she'd wear on stage.

Jo takes about ten minutes. When she sees the result, Victoria is convinced that Jo's drawn in some wrinkles. It's not a transformation, but she does look a few years older, and that might be enough to convince the judges.

The judges see everyone at least once during the morning. They've identified a few people who are definitely going through to the next stage, and some that have definitely reached the end of the line.

In the afternoon, there's a surprise guest. Lisa Riley, who played Mandy Dingle in *Emmerdale* for six years, arrives for a short question-and-answer session. The brief is to ask her about screen kisses, because the kissing scene is coming up. Lisa's advice is, 'Stay off the garlic. Take the other actor to one side and ask them how you'll do it, so there are no surprises. Do not feel vain.'

She's asked what her real boyfriend thinks. She quickly asserts that she doesn't have a boyfriend (winking to them), but tells them it's the job she does and he understands that. The questions soon stray into more general territory, and it's an interesting insight into what the hopefuls are worried about. How will the cast of *Emmerdale* react to the *Soapstars* winners? Lisa can't see that they'd have any problems. What are directors looking for in a performance? Do the actors get any say about their 'image'? What should they do if they don't get it? Her advice is encouraging: 'Never, ever give up hope. For three years I never got the role, but there are jobs for all of us out there. Never let anyone hurt you, either.'

One of Lisa's answers in particular gets the hopefuls thinking. As soon as she appeared on *Emmerdale*, the tabloids started writing stories about her. An ex-boyfriend sold a kiss-and-tell story, from behind prison bars. If that wasn't bad enough, one paper hung around outside the hospital where Lisa's mother was being treated for breast cancer, apparently seeing some entertainment value in doing so.

Afterwards, the hopefuls are mulling this over. They know how the tabloids work – most admit that they enjoy reading at least some form of celebrity gossip. Almost everyone here is very media-savvy. The winners will find themselves under the same scrutiny as the *Popstars* winners did. And some of the other finalists will also find their private lives under the microscopes. At the moment, it's still a month before the first *Soapstars* programme is broadcast, but once the show's on the air, people are realistic – the contestants in *Big Brother 2* and *Survivor* have had stories printed about them. It might well happen to the *Soapstars* winners.

At this stage, it's interesting that very few of the hopefuls want 'fame' in itself. It's a marked contrast to the fame-hungry crowds at the open auditions. People seem motivated by all sorts of things:

- *'I get a real buzz from being on stage. I feel more alive up there.'*

- *'It's hard work, I want the challenge.'*

- *'I'm on income support, I come from a poor family. I want my kid to have more opportunities than I did.'*

- *'I'm ready for it. I've reached a point in my life where I want to change.'*

Most see fame as an unfortunate side-effect of success as a TV actor, but they appreciate that it 'goes with the territory'. Lisa Riley's experience has worried a lot of them – mainly because they may also be dragging their families into the public eye.

Some of the semi-finalists have had a wild or troubled past. A couple of them are open about it. Johnny Kinch was kicked out of RADA. He's had gambling problems, lost everything and lived rough for two years. He's still only thirty, but he's rebuilt his life and the experience has ultimately made him stronger, more appreciative of the opportunity he has now. He knows the papers could find out, but sees it as a good thing – he's got nothing to hide. He already does charity work for gambling addiction organizations. Fame on *Emmerdale* might mean higher awareness for the cause, so some good may come of it. In the short term, he's used his experiences to inform his improvisation in the first round, and it's got him through this far.

Most of the hopefuls, though, think the tabloids will struggle to find a front-page headline about them:

- *'I don't even drink, let alone do drugs.'*

- *'I'm the most boring person on the planet.'*

– *'My partner's just had major bowel surgery, how about that?'*

They all retain a healthy cynicism towards the tabloid press, though – if there isn't a story, the papers will just make one up. A few have got friends or families who are journalists, and they spell it out – if the papers decide you're newsworthy, they'll dig up old boyfriends and girlfriends. And they'll pay for stories and pictures – not just embarrassing 'before they were famous' shots of school plays and bad hair days, but shots of them on holiday or at drunken parties.

The hopefuls go quiet, remembering some of the stories they've read. Minor indiscretions could become a big deal. Getting caught nicking a Mars Bar as a kid, losing your virginity at fifteen, smoking a joint once, having sex outside, even throwing up at a party. Take any ordinary office – you'll find people who did those things, and very few people who'd see any great harm in them. But the papers might see any of those as newsworthy if it happened to someone *famous*. One of the men admits to having a couple of wild years as a teen, and a few people – including a couple of teens – nod in recognition. One girl has just split up with her boyfriend, and it wasn't on good terms. They were together for a couple of years, they did the normal things that couples do. She can't be sure he wouldn't sell his story, and isn't encouraged by the idea that the more detail he goes into and pictures of her he's willing to hand over, the more money he'll get. She's done nothing wrong, or even unusual, but he's still got a few Polaroids of her that would sell newspapers.

Another girl relaxes a bit. The nearest she's got to that is a picture of herself wrapped up in a towel – her boyfriend liked her legs. It's a picture she'd be happy for

> ### TIM WORSNOP, *Emmerdale*'s chief press officer
>
> 'People will come out of the woodwork – be they ex-partners or one-time "friends".'

people to see. One of the others pipes up – what if they stuck a caption over the towel, to make it look like she was naked? What if they just faked a nude photo from it? One of the teenaged girls smiles – she doesn't think there's even a holiday snap of her in a swimming costume. She's never had a boyfriend. The others take a deep breath – '*Soapstars Girl Still A Virgin*', one of them says, blocking out an imaginary headline with his hand. Even leading a blameless life is newsworthy. You can't win.

It's a sobering thought, but one that has occurred to most of the hopefuls at some point in the last few weeks. The weird thing, they agree, is that the tabloids will get interested in *some of the people in this room, right now*. At some point, most of them will cross a line, become *famous*, become (as the papers see it) a legitimate target.

Tim Worsnop is the *Emmerdale*'s Chief Press Officer at Yorkshire TV, the man whose job it is to liaise with the press. He knows full well that the *Soapstars* winners will be 'newsworthy', and that the press will find stories about them.

'When new people are thrust into the limelight there is an immediate market for stories about them, and usually because there is money to be made, no shortage of people willing to sell those stories,' Tim explains. 'On a more down-to-earth level, local freelance journalists will no doubt be combing the area people come from, to see if there is a story they can market. In all cases the better the story, the more money there is to make.

'It is interesting to see how people handle press interest in them. Some people are naturally very good at it, with a seemingly endless supply of stories and opinions that journalists crave. Other people have to work very hard at their relationships with the press. What we try to do is introduce artists, particularly those who are previously inexperienced in these matters, as gently as possible. On occasions we'd carry out mock interviews to prepare them. Not all stories papers chase are negative, but clearly those are the ones that would concern us the most.

'National papers would, as a rule, contact us prior to a story appearing, firstly out of courtesy because we all do lots of work together, and secondly, although not on every occasion, to seek a comment on behalf of the show.

'Over the years there have been plenty of kiss-and-tell stories about actors in the show. Unfortunately for them, it is part and parcel of being in the spotlight. We are always there to help and unless lawyers are involved we would act as intermediaries between the publication and the person concerned. There are ways of tackling certain types of stories from a PR point of view but those must remain trade secrets.

'On occasions where artists or the show feels it has been hard done to we might seek recourse from the Press Complaints Commission. We recently won a PCC case and have no qualms calling on them if we feel we have been badly treated. And, of course, if it is something the company views as particularly serious we would employ the services not only of our own lawyers, but the company of specialist media lawyers who act on our behalf in these circumstances.'

While the hopefuls think about the downside of fame, the judges are deliberating about who will be taking the

next step towards it. The original plan was to get down to
about fifty by the end of the day, but the judges are starting
to wonder if they could lose a few more. If half the seventy-
two people went today, they could spend more time
concentrating on the remaining half, instead of wasting
time seeing people that they knew they would be losing at
the end of the second day. The change is agreed, but it
leads to an hour's delay as the judges confer.

They like Jo-Ann D'Costa – 'She's like a muppet,' Bill
says, 'but she's a lovely muppet.' 'She's a little muppet, we
love her,' Yvon agrees, neither of them realizing that when
their remarks are broadcast, Jo-Ann's friends will have a
field day.

They also like Erin Lordan. 'One of the few mums we've
got whom I think I could write "sexy" for,' Bill says. And as
for Dee Whitehead: 'She's terrific.' They keep working
down their lists. At this stage, there's not a huge amount of
dissent – Yvon's still not sure about Ashra, thinking the
make-up she's had to make her look younger has made her
look even older, but agrees she's a good enough actress to
go through. Yvon's marked Johnny Kinch down as a potential winner. Bill wants to see him go through, but thinks it's
premature to declare it's in the bag for him.

Back in the studio, the mood of the hopefuls changes.
It's a hot day, the air's quite dry, and they've been here for
almost ten hours. They begin to suspect that the long delay
is some sort of psychological game on the part of the
programme makers. People are becoming more subdued,
as they realize the moment of decision is approaching.

The judges eventually return to the hall, and a hush
falls. They tell the hopefuls that they'll be divided into two
groups – one's to go to the left of the studio floor, the other

to the right. Paul begins calling out names. People make their way down, standing quietly on one side or the other. Everyone's guessed that one group will be going through, the other one will be going home. But no one's quite sure which group is which. With more than seventy names to call out, the process takes a few minutes. Even towards the end, no one's entirely sure whether they're through. The group to the right is looking a little happier than the group on the left, though. And they are right to – they are the thirty-four people going through.

Radio presenter Becky hasn't made it. She's not too devastated, and doubts she'll try her hand at acting again. A few people are upset, but most are stoical – it really was an achievement to get this far, and '*Soapstars* semi-finalist' will look good on a CV. Many liken it to an acting workshop more than an audition. A lot of people have made friends and are frantically exchanging addresses. The winners are, naturally enough, elated. At the same time, it's been a long day, and there are potentially two more to go.

Inside the studio it's been easy to lose track of time. When people arrived this morning, it was a sunny summer's day. As they leave, it's something of a surprise to emerge in the middle of a rainstorm.

day two

Thirty-four surviving hopefuls arrive at a new, smaller venue, the LWT rehearsal rooms in Kennington, South London. In the next room, as people will discover as the day goes on, Kathy Burke and James Dreyfus are busy rehearsing a new episode of *Gimme Gimme Gimme*. The group is in good spirits – they were given a couple of scripts to learn overnight, one from *Coronation Street*, one from *Cold Feet*, but most still found enough time last night to meet up in the bar, or have a meal with other hopefuls.

Thirty-three have made it this far:

☐ (The mum of the family) – Sally Austen, Debbie Dawson, Vicki Greenwood, Erin Lordan, Debra Michaels, Sarah Smart, Victoria Tonge and Dee Whitehead.

☐ (The dad of the family) – Chris Burdett, Daz Crawford, Mark Jardine, Johnny Kinch, Paul McCarthy and Brian McDevitt.

☐ (The son) – Dean Abrahams, Dean Cook, Jason Hain, Craig Henderson, Asta Philpott, Adrian Russell and Anthony Spillane.

☐ (The elder daughter) – Ruth Abram, Ide Chiahmen, Catherine Jordan, Nicola Orr and Ashra Price.

☐ (The younger daughter) – Becky Armory, Gemma Baker, Elspeth Brodie, Katie Heppel, Daniella Pattinson, Emma Pollard and Becky Weeks.

Jo-Ann D'Costa has fallen ill overnight. The judges are unanimous – she's certainly good enough to make it through to the final, based on what they've seen. The others don't have it so easy....

By now, almost everyone left in has previous acting experience or some formal training or qualification. Most of the people remaining have at least some professional acting credits, many – even the teenagers – have been in the business for years.

For example, Erin Lordan has worked extensively on the stage all over the world, in productions such as *Cats* and *Starlight Express*, and has released an album of dance music. At sixteen, she was a member of Hot Gossip. She's the daughter of Jerry Lordan, who wrote songs for The Shadows, including 'Apache'.

Daz Crawford has been a model and has appeared in action films such as *The World is Not Enough* and *Blade 2*, but his greatest claim to fame to date is that he was Diesel in *Gladiators*.

Dean Cook is the boy from the Yellow Pages advert who stands on the directory to reach up to kiss a girl – he made the advert eight years ago, and it's run every Christmas since. If he had been an adult actor at the time, he could practically have retired on the proceeds. As it is, he's had to keep working, and has racked up an impressive CV – appearing in the films *The Little Vampire* and *Plunkett and Macleane*, as well as other commercials.

Ashra Price has been an extra in *Pobol y Cwm* and *Border Café*, and had a small speaking part in *Nuts and Bolts*. She's recently finished a BTEC drama course. She reached the Birmingham semi-final of *Popstars*, and she was one of the contestants in the *Weakest Link Welsh Special*.

Becky Weeks is a trained dancer and singer, who has appeared in a film, *The Ghost of Greville Lodge*, with Prunella Scales, which will be shown on television in autumn 2001. She's also appeared in *Galileo's Ghost*, *Mike & Angelo* and *Paradise* on television as well as doing work for radio and commercials. She's worked extensively on the stage, including *The Darling Buds of May*, *The Ragged Child* and *Nutcracker and the Mouse King*.

Others have been singers or stand-up comedians. Some of the younger ones are still at school, or have recently completed acting courses. There's no one left who's just walked in off the street with no previous dramatic or performance experience or training at all. The closest to a complete newcomer is possibly Vicki Greenwood, who's been a member of an amateur dramatics group for a few months, but doesn't have any formal training.

In the morning, the hopefuls run through short scripts again – this time, the scenes are from *Coronation Street*. Rather than being paired off in advance, they don't know who their 'partner' will be this time round. It means they have to find a way to work together, to accommodate each other's styles, in the performance itself. The standard of performance is markedly better than it had been even the day before. With a few exceptions. Mark Jardine:

'It was most tense for me in the semis, not the finals. One of the people who came in to talk to us had told us that actors couldn't screw up, because all eyes were on us. We had a really tense scene that afternoon, anyway – the Ken confronting Deirdre one. I really had to let rip, and I thought I had to do that anyway, because up until then I was very conscious I was Mr Nice, and wasn't really showing my range. So it was a tense atmosphere anyway, we'd been told not to screw up, I had everything to prove, and I was with Sarah, who'd got something of a reputation for blowing her lines, and she did it again with me ... so it was a powder keg, really. I felt really wound up, so I thought I'd use it, and I really let rip. And halfway through, I heard one of the judges going "He's overacting ... he's awful", and of course that was the one bit they showed on the telly.'

The judges' nerves are settled a bit – it's clear that

almost all the people here could be good enough. It's also clear that there are at least a couple of contenders for all the parts. At the same time, there's no one head and shoulders above the rest of the pack – from what they've seen so far, it's too early to say they've discovered any shining stars of the future. As Bill puts it, 'I'd have some of these people in *Emmerdale*, but I wouldn't let any of them marry my daughter.'

The morning passes smoothly – everyone's mastered their lines, and seems relaxed and confident. Ruth, called on to slap Debra as part of her scene gets a little carried away and almost knocks her down to the floor.

Ashra Price and Dee Whitehead are sent off to rehearse a scene together. The judges have them earmarked as a potential mother and daughter pair. Ashra, at twenty-six, is an 'in-betweener' – too old to be a teenaged daughter, too young to be the mother of a teenaged daughter. She's only a couple of years younger than Victoria Tonge and Vicki Greenwood, two of the hopeful mums, and they would struggle to make the relationship convincing. Yvon's not been convinced by Ashra from the beginning, but Dee's old enough to really be Ashra's mum, and both are blonde with blue eyes, and have the same shaped face. Physically, they could be mother and daughter. Ashra laughs – she looks more like her dad, and her real mum is dark-haired. Dee's got two teenage sons, but no daughter. 'I'm pleased to be doing a scene with mother and daughter – all my scenes until now, right from my first audition, have been me arguing with my husband.' As it turns out, the scene has her arguing with her daughter when she discovers she's pregnant. But Ashra and Dee are both happy with their performances, and the judges are nodding at each other.

The *Soapstars* crew is kept busy filming not just the performances and the judges' reaction, but also mini-interviews with the semi-finalists. Morale among the hopefuls is very high. There are a few people who think they've done badly and are on their way out. One of those is Erin Lordan – but when pressed, she admits that assuming she's failed is her way of coping with the possibility of rejection. Most people are still pleased to have got this far.

For the afternoon session, the judges have a couple of surprises up their sleeves. The hopefuls are led away in groups, and told that there's been a change of plan – instead of performing the *Cold Feet* scene they were given to memorize the night before, there's another scene to learn.

And they're on in ten minutes.

It's the sort of thing that might happen on a soap. If an actor who's needed for a scene is stuck on a train, or ill, or a certain set isn't ready, or the weather is wrong, the rest of the cast wouldn't stand around waiting, they'd get on with another scene. This, the judges think, will be a test that separates the wheat from the chaff. It's not just about learning lines in a short space of time (itself no mean feat), it's about interpreting those lines. The hopefuls will have to cope with the stress. It's been a long couple of days, but no longer than the days will be in the *Emmerdale* studio. And as if all that wasn't enough, the scenes are the first outright humorous ones the hopefuls have had to deal with. So the judges will also be assessing comic timing and delivery.

You'd think at least some of the hopefuls would just pack it in there and then. But they all relish the challenge. Brian McDevitt sums it up: 'We're in gear, we've been using our acting muscles for two days solid.' The fact it's a comedy script makes it easier, it seems, to remember the lines, to spark off your partner.

Everyone passes the test, some with flying colours. Special mention has to go to sixteen-year-old Emma Pollard, who despite going down with a sore throat, puts in a sterling performance in the part of Adam, normally played by James Nesbitt, who's more than twice her age. She's not happy with how she did, but the other hopefuls cheer her, and the panel are impressed.

With the auditions done, the judges meet up behind closed doors. It's half an hour before the group are called back in. Solemnly, Bill tells them it's been a very hard decision. Then, as has become the tradition, he tells people to come up when their name is called, and either go to his right or his left. The mood of the hopefuls is suddenly a lot more sombre. Particularly when it becomes clear that the groups are about the same size. If 'left' was for 'loser' yesterday, does it mean the same thing today, or have they switched it round? Whatever the case, a lot of people are going home, it seems. As Bill reaches the end of his list, no one's quite sure how they've done – there are some good people in both groups. Some very good people. The hopefuls are tense, taking deep breaths, looking nervously at the people they are standing next to, and those across the room.

Bill announces that everyone's done really well.

He hesitates.

Everyone's done so well, in fact, that everyone's coming back tomorrow.

The hopefuls pause, then what Bill just said sinks in. After two days of having to call up emotions to order, they suddenly find themselves caught out, and all sorts of feelings just flood out. Stunned silence gives away to a sigh of relief, disbelief, nervous laughter and tears of joy at getting through. Within a few seconds a lot of the hopefuls are joining in with Bill, who's laughing his head off. Although a few are of a mind to re-enact the slapping scene from the morning.

The crew were in on the joke. When it became clear that everyone was doing well, and the judges were loathe to lose anyone, Tim Miller was worried that letting everyone through wouldn't be dramatic enough for the TV programme – this was meant to be a real moment of decision. Between them, Bill and he cooked up the joke, to create a little drama.

Bill's still laughing. '*That's* comic timing,' he chuckles.

The young girls are sitting on the front row, arms crossed, mock-sulking.

– *'He's horrible.'*

– *'Look at him smiling.'*

– *'He's a bastard.'*

– *'I bet he's just like that at home.'*

A few minutes later, the hopefuls have calmed down, and it's sunk in – everyone in the room has a real chance of making it to the final. Most of the people here now have done far better than they'd expected. They've come a long way – but now they're much too close to the finals, and winning those, to be content with resting on their laurels.

There's also the recognition that there's another day to go.

day three

Monday morning, back at the LWT rehearsal rooms. A few of the hopefuls have hastily phoned in sick to work, using all their acting skills to persuade their bosses they're feeling ill. Others don't have to act – yesterday, a couple of the hopefuls had sore throats. Today, about half of them do. Whether it's a bug, or just the hot weather, no one's sure.

Becky Armory isn't here. She's dropped out, having accepted the offer of a run in the West End, in *Caught in the Net*, Ray Cooney's sequel to *Run for Your Wife*, and today she's recording an episode of *Harry and Cosh*, a Channel Five series in which she's got a regular part. Yesterday evening she told Paul, and was very tearful. Paul reassured her that *Soapstars* was about finding actors work – she shouldn't be upset to be working. She promises to stay in touch with him.

Today, for the first time, the hopefuls are told about the parts that are available, and read the short character descriptions. The judges are quick to reiterate to all the hopefuls that they can be a little bit older or younger than specified. If the final family isn't all from the same ethnic group, or there's some other way in which they stand out (one tall, thin one in a family of short, fat ones, for example, or one Mancunian in a family with Scots accents), then there's room to explain that they're adopted. The final family will have to gel, to be a convincing family. And, at some level, they will have to look right together. But, by definition, anyone who is here is in with a real chance.

It's usually obvious which actor is going for which part, but there are a couple of 'in-betweeners', like Victoria Tonge and Craig Henderson. At this stage the judges make a decision – Victoria is being considered for the mum of the family; Craig's the son.

The previous two days have been long and they've been hard work. Today is another hot day, although it's a lighter schedule. For the first time, the hopefuls are being organized into families. This serves two purposes – first, it gives the judges the chance to see the whole family together. At the end of every piece, they get the hopefuls to shuffle around on the sofa, and watch their monitors closely – they sit 'mothers' and 'fathers' together, then pair them up with their 'children'. The real work matching up families will come at the finals, but the judges know they have to do at least some groundwork here, because they don't want to rule out anyone they might need. The second purpose is perhaps more fundamental. Up until now, all the scenes have been two-handers, so this is the first time the judges have seen the actors working within a larger group. It's not a massive challenge, but it does mean the actors have to carefully pitch their performances, to fit in with the other people in the scene, not just match up with one other actor.

Events have caught up with Dee. For two days she's been concentrating on her performance, and impressing the judges. But today is the day of her father's funeral. She's chosen to be here, instead. At one of the breaks, she starts crying. A couple of the other semi-finalists know what's happened, and comfort her. But, as the hour of the funeral approaches, Dee's become very upset. Tim Miller, the judges and the *Soapstars* crew don't have any idea about Dee's circumstances. Unknown to Dee, she's already one of a handful whom all three judges agree have almost certainly made it through to the finals.

When Tim finally discovers that Dee is missing her father's funeral, he is horrified – he quickly calls a halt to proceedings and chats to Dee in private. She can't stay here, they call up a taxi, and book her onto the first train home to Nottingham. While they wait for that, the judges tell her things are looking good, and they'll soon call her. The judges had no idea, and had caught no hint, of her situation. They were impressed already by the performance; now she's gone up another few notches in their estimation. Dee doesn't get home in time for the service, but does get the chance to meet friends and relatives afterwards. By then, Paul has phoned her to say that she is through to the next round.

There's a long lunchbreak. The *Soapstars* crew take the opportunity to record interviews with all of the semi-finalists here. The hopefuls congregate in another rehearsal room... and they are starting to get a bit tense. They know that most of them will get through, but they still aren't entirely sure what criteria the judges are using. A lot of them are tired, and the sore throats are taking their toll. A good test is that very few of them are sure what day it is – the first day of auditions was Saturday, so this is Sunday... no, hang on, Tuesday. There's good team spirit, tinged with the knowledge that it's not long before they could find out that, after all that, they won't be going any further.

The judges are looking to lose nine people. There's no quota, but they are hoping to get down to five people for each of the roles. As it happens, when they compare notes, they've got exactly that. The decisions are getting harder to make, but a few people have had enough chances to prove themselves by now and still haven't reached the level of consistency they'll need.

At this level, they want to talk to everyone face-to-face. While it will be no consolation, they want to give some advice to people that won't make it through, because they really were very close. They've also got concerns about a few of the finalists – mostly, people are told to watch soaps, British TV dramas and films, to see the style of perform-ance. Others are told to work on specific areas – they're better at arguments than comedy, say, or they've got a tendency to over- or underplay. The most common advice is 'Bring it down a little bit'.

In the other room, the hopefuls are tense as their names are called out in alphabetical order, and they make their way one by one to the judges. They're aware of the maths – if you're auditioning for the part of the son, then the more of the other 'sons' that get through, the less your chances. Some of those who haven't made it don't want to face the hall, and go straight home. Others go back in for hugs and words of support. Those that get through are, of course, elated. Even the most confident, relaxed hopeful can't be sure what the judges will tell them. Emma Pollard and Erin Lordan keep almost bumping into each other as they pace around, waiting for the summons. Many of the others prefer to sit quietly, keeping track of whose name is being called. Most of the hopefuls have talked themselves into thinking the worst – that way, they figure, they can only be pleasantly surprised. Some of them have started grumbling about the cameras – they don't want people to point cameras at them; they don't want their private feel-ings to become entertainment.

It's tough work for the judges, none of whom relishes being the bearer of bad news. They take it in turns – but as chance would have it, it always seems to fall to Bill to turn people down. He puts a brave face on it, but he admits he doesn't enjoy telling any of the hopefuls that they've reached the end of the line, particularly the teenagers.

Johnny Kinch is through. He strolls back into the other room and punches the air. 'WHO'S THE DADDY?' he roars. The judges hear him through two allegedly sound-proof doors and chuckle.

Asta Philpott, a boy in a wheelchair, who's been keeping up everyone's morale all weekend, even giving people rides in his chair, hasn't made it. The judges were surprised that someone so naturally funny wasn't a natural at his comedy scene. When the bad news emerges, even some of the crew are in tears.

Ashra Price and Dee Whitehead are through.

Nicola Orr is through, though the judges have a huge reservation – she's a redhead who looks nothing like any of the parents. Paul wants her in because 'she's so bloody good', and the other judges concur.

Victoria Tonge isn't through. The judges tell her something she'd suspected anyway – she wasn't old enough for the part. She's a good actress and they want to encourage her, but, after three days of mulling it over, they've concluded she wasn't right for this.

Those that aren't through are:
- [ ] Sally Austen
- [ ] Chris Burdett
- [ ] Katie Heppel
- [ ] Catherine Jordan
- [ ] Asta Philpott
- [ ] Sarah Smart
- [ ] Anthony Spillaine
- [ ] Victoria Tonge

And, after about an hour, the semi-finals are over. Twenty-three of them line up for the cameras (Jo-Ann D'Costa is ill, Dee Whitehead has returned home). The cameras sweep along the line, and the hopefuls are in bullish mood. They're finalists, now, and whatever happens, they can all expect to get exposure on national TV. Whatever happens, they've proved they've got what it takes.

getting serious now

CHAPTER FIVE

Tuesday 28 August, 2001. The start of the finals: twenty-four finalists face the Emmerdale *producers for the first time.*

day one

The finalists have come to Leeds, fresh for the week-long finals. By the end of the week, the judges will have narrowed it down to just ten people – two for each available role. This week is designed to show how the hopefuls cope with a variety of different challenges, and will also see them coached by a couple of directors, meet an actor from *Emmerdale*, and see a couple of the locations that they'd be working in, if they make it. Mostly, they'll be based at the Trinity and All Saints College in Horsforth, about halfway between the *Emmerdale* studios in Leeds and the Emmerdale village set. The college is a typical campus site – concrete residential blocks, winding corridors, canteens and bars. It's a couple of weeks before term starts, and there's only a skeleton staff, some builders and a small conference party here, so the *Soapstars* have the place almost to themselves.

Twenty-four *Soapstars* hopefuls are here. A couple of the group have had an attack of nerves at some point in the last three weeks, and considered not showing up. In the end, only Daz Crawford has dropped out, after accepting a part in a film. The remaining four dads aren't sure what the implications are. Mark thinks 'It's shortened the odds, so we've got more chance statistically, so it's got to be good news.' Brian's conclusion is 'It means we'll have more of a chance to prove ourselves, so it should help us.'

So, the following actors are up for the following parts:

❑ 'Dads' – Mark Jardine, Johnny Kinch, Paul McCarthy, Brian McDevitt.

❑ 'Mums' – Debbie Dawson, Vicki Greenwood, Erin Lordan, Debra Michaels, Dee Whitehead.

❑ 'Sons' – Dean Abrahams, Dean Cook, Jason Hain, Craig Henderson, Adrian Russell.

❑ 'Elder daughters' – Ruth Abram, Elspeth Brodie, Ide Chiahmen, Nicola Orr, Ashra Price.

❑ 'Younger daughters' – Gemma Baker, Jo-Ann D'Costa, Danielle Pattinson, Emma Pollard, Becky Weeks.

At this level, it seems there's very little to choose between the remaining actors.

Debra Michaels has extensive theatre experience, most recently including *Soul Train*, *Trickster's Payback* and *Sleeping Beauty*. She played Carmen Jones in a production that toured Europe. She also has TV experience – she played a regular role in the ITV children's series *The Lodge*.

Johnny Kinch works as a compere and stand-up comedian. Ten years ago, he was kicked out of RADA, following which he had problems with alcohol and gambling. He managed to lose a fingertip in a fight with a chef. Now he's rebuilt his life, and drawn strength from his experiences. He's had a few acting roles, most notably in the British film *Out of Depth*, where he got to stab Sean Maguire to death.

Craig Henderson was born in Edinburgh, and now divides his time between London and Los Angeles. His CV is quite something. Craig's got a Masters in Classical Archaeology from the University of Edinburgh and studied at RADA, The Actors Institute and the Groundlings School of Improvisation in Los Angeles. He's appeared in many commercials, played the lead in *The Quarry Men*, a British film directed by Toby White, and the part of astronaut Richard Goodchild in CNN's series *A History of the Future*. Craig has worked as an artist, and had three paintings published as limited editions. He has skied for the army, represented his country in the military pentathlon, and ran 200 metres and 400 metres for Hampshire and Edinburgh University. He's also worked as a stuntman.

For the last two years, Gemma Baker has been a regular in the Channel Five series *Harry and Cosh*, playing Kimberly Palmer.

Jo-Ann D'Costa lives in Sussex. At nineteen, she got a job at KISS FM. She voiced radio adverts for KISS and Capital, and before long was presenting vox pops for KISS TV. After a year, she decided to study Performing Arts at the University of Luton – a three-year course, for which she earned a first. At university she acted in several adverts for Trouble TV, doing celebrity interviews. From that, she was snapped up by MTV, where she worked as a floor manager on MTV Select. Jo-Ann auditioned for a presenter's job on E4's *Popworld*, getting down to the last two, but she wasn't chosen. She was one of 3,000 applicants to be the new CITV presenter – again, she got down to the last two. She's had to make a difficult decision – the CITV final is the same week as the one for *Soapstars*. Jo-Ann's chosen to be here.

The judges are keeping their options open with the daughters, though – Elspeth and Ide are being considered for both roles. If it came to it, there would be enough flexibility to allow any two of the ten young women to get the parts.

There are a number of anomalies, now – three of the 'mums' don't have kids, two of the 'daughters' do. Ashra Price is the eldest of the 'daughters' – she's ten years older than the youngest 'daughter', and only three years younger than the youngest 'mum' and 'dad'. Elspeth is down to play the eldest daughter, but she's younger than three of the 'younger daughters'.

While the crew set up, the hopefuls bunch into groups outside reception, and some of them chat to the judges. Almost all of them came over the previous evening, and the spirit of camaraderie that was evident at the semis is still there. A number of them have met up in the last couple of weeks, and they've stayed in touch by phone. The mums are the most chummy – Debbie Dawson and Debra Michaels in particularly seem inseparable. They've been given a couple of scripts to learn, and they've been given a vague idea of what's in store for them this week.

Emma Pollard had her GCSE results the previous week, and says they were OK. Johnny Kinch has got himself an agent, and straight away has signed up to do an advert for Matalan. A few of the others have arranged agents for themselves, or had new publicity photos done. Many already had agents. The response to *Soapstars* from agents has been mixed – some have told the actors on their books to stay away, others have pushed them to the auditions, particularly the adult audition in London. One of the 'dads' went to an open audition, against his agent's advice, and is now through to the final. His conclusion is that he shouldn't listen to his agent so much in future. Although the show will soon be on the air, few of the finalists have given much thought as to how they'll exploit their exposure on primetime TV, although pretty well all of them are hoping that they'll be spotted and get work off the back of it, assuming they don't win.

Erin Lordan sums up a common experience – 'I was so excited to get through to the finals that I couldn't sleep for a week after the semis – and I've been so nervous about the finals that I've not slept for the last week, either.' While a few of the group seem nonchalant, the hopefuls are averaging five or six hours' sleep a night. Morale has been improved with the news that no one will be going home tonight – the judges will whittle the group down to fifteen, but tomorrow, not today as originally planned, with a further five going on the Thursday night. But now they are here, it's starting to hit home just how few of them are left, how close they are to a part on *Emmerdale*... and just how tough the competition is.

The judges are happy. After what seemed like an unpromising start, they're down to a group where they are almost spoiled for choice. Paul circulates, giving people career advice and – to some of them, anyway – the numbers of agents he thinks will be able to help them. Bill's convinced that out of the twenty-four people, twenty of them could be good enough to be in the show, and, if they're able to exploit the opportunity, will go on to bigger and better things. By now, the judges are getting on well with the hopefuls, and are chatting to them during some of the breaks. The *Soapstars* crew are also now on first-name terms with the finalists. Despite that, a couple of the finalists, Elspeth Brodie and Becky Weeks, are still wearing their number badges as lucky charms.

The first episode of the *Soapstars* programme is going to be broadcast on the following Monday 3 September. It's on straight after an extended edition of *Coronation Street*, but that means it's not starting until 9.30pm. It's later than the crew would have liked – they're worried that a lot of the kids who would normally watch will be in bed. Pleased with the rough cuts of the early episodes, the network have ordered two more half-hour shows. In addition to that, ITV2 have ordered a whole series of *Soapstars Extra* programmes, each an hour long, offering the opportunity to go into greater depth than the ITV1 half-hour shows. There will also be a special show profiling the judges, and *Nearly Soapstars*, which goes back to visit the more memorable people who didn't make it. It's extra work for an already very busy team. Back in London, there are now nine editing suites working simultaneously to put the shows together in time. Tim Miller will spend a lot of this week on his mobile, coordinating the effort.

'It's hectic because of the large numbers of people involved in each production,' he confesses. 'I've got several bosses; my executive producer at LWT, *Emmerdale's* producers, the commissioning editor at ITV, producers higher up in the Granada food chain. In addition, there are the website people, the book people, the press office, the promos department.'

The five 'youngest daughters' pose together for a photo, which looks for all the world like a rehearsal for the cover of the December issue of *FHM*. It's still not sunk in that millions of people will be watching them in less than a week. The hopefuls now know that there will be two half-hour shows just dedicated to this week's final, but most are still convinced that unless they win they'll barely be glimpsed. Over the weekend, at the Guardian Edinburgh TV Festival, psychologist Dr Oliver James said he feared that people could actually be 'damaged' by taking part in programmes such as *Big Brother* and *Temptation Island*. Having spoken to some contestants, he felt they were not aware of the impact their participation would have on their lives. The previous week, Darren from *Big Brother 2* explained what it was like on the chat show *This Week Only*:

> 'It's very, very odd, because I'm just a completely ordinary bloke who seems to have had like a fame button switched on – everyone knows me, everywhere I go, and it is a bit unusual. But it's not particularly harrowing or bad.'

The vast majority of the finalists don't seem to realize that their 'fame buttons' are about to be switched on, that they'll be stopped in the street, and that the papers will become extremely interested in them. They understand the nature of *Soapstars*, and they've all seen shows such as *Big Brother* and *Popstars*, which, of course, comes closest of all to the format they're experiencing. Most of the girls seem to relish the idea that they could soon be getting calls to appear in *Loaded* or *FHM*. Ruth Abram's up for it if they

> **TIM MILLER, *Soapstars* producer**
>
> 'Everyone wants to know about *Soapstars*. Everyone wants tapes. Because we're cutting the programmes close to transmission, this is a bit of a nightmare.'

ask, saying that she sees it as part of the process for an actress these days. Nicola Orr and Ashra Price have both had babies in the last six months, so they're sceptical they'll be asked, but Nicola also jokes about airbrushes, and seems keen. None of them really believes that their picture could be used to sell papers.

Was it deliberate that the finals would be over before the actors got to see themselves on TV? Tim admits it's 'a happy coincidence. If people could see what they look like, and what the judges are saying, just having the show running would have affected them.' As it is, the listings magazines have come out, and many feature articles about the series – at this stage, they concentrate on 'Evil Yvon' and the more deluded hopefuls at the fifteen-second stage of the open auditions. That seems like a very long time ago now to the finalists, and they're a little annoyed that the coverage is talking about people 'coming in off the street'. When people see the second half of the series, they hope the audience will realize that it's actually been hard work. Elspeth Brodie is reading her copy of *Heat,* when she turns a page and finds a two-page article on the series. Everyone crowds around to get a look, to see if they or anyone they know are in any of the pictures (apart from the judges, they don't recognize anyone). Vicki Greenwood's seen herself in a TV trailer for the series, giving someone a good slap. She's one of only three finalists with no professional acting experience, and has never seen herself on TV before. She's also told Tim Miller that she's resigned from her job at a bank. 'He was horrified,' Vicki laughs, 'a bit of a giveaway I'm not going to get it, don't you think? I told him I didn't think I'd won, I just wasn't enjoying working at a bank'.

There's another surprise for the finalists – the judges have been joined by Steve Frost and Keith Richardson, the producer and executive producer of *Emmerdale*. Steve had attended the semi-final, without announcing his presence to the hopefuls. None of the finalists recognizes him from then. Both he and Keith have kept in close touch with the process, especially from the semi-final stage, when the numbers were more manageable – they've seen photos and videos of the most promising candidates. They don't have any direct control over the selection, but their opinion is clearly an important factor for the judges to bear in mind, as these are the people who will have to work with the winners. Keith and Bill Lyons are old friends, and on a couple of occasions they take the opportunity to sneak off to compare notes.

The presence of the producers ups the ante for the finalists. The stakes have just got higher for Jo-Ann. 'It's brought it home how close we are. But it's like we've got to start again, they won't know how we've done up to now. We've got to prove ourselves again, and not make any mistakes.' Ruth agrees – 'It's quite scary, really, because the producers are here. We've got to know Bill, Paul and Yvon, but these guys are the big cheeses.' For Dee, it makes every-thing seem more real: 'You think about all the talent and the people they work with normally, and you think "Are they really here to look at little old me?"'

The finalists convene in The Blue Room, a lecture hall. It's a warm day, but not as stifling as it had been at the semi-finals. The first order of business is familiar territory by now – a run-through of the *Emmerdale* scenes they've been given to learn the previous night. They all slip back into playing Sean and Angie or Marc and Ollie easily. A few of them have to overcome nerves, a few lines are missed. At this stage, this worries the hopefuls far more than the judges. Johnny Kinch admits later, 'I thought I was dreadful – I dropped a line, today of all days.' Steve and Keith watch the proceedings from the judges' table for the first time, making their own notes. Both agree that the overall standard is very high.

The hopefuls are now given a new scene, the first one they've seen with the characters they'll be playing. It's actually the very first scene that will be broadcast, and the winners will be performing it for real in a little over a month's time. Phil and Maggie's cars have bumped into each other, and Scott Windsor, the local mechanic, has come to their rescue:

[Phil gets out of his car and walks angrily to confront Maggie. Lucy, Craig and Jess – with Brad the dog (name tbc) follow them out. They are almost in front of the garage]

PHIL: *What the hell were you playing at?*

LUCY: *You could have killed us.*

JESS: *Never mind that, what about Brad?*

[She strokes him]

MAGGIE: *You were too close.*

PHIL: *How did I know you were going to stop like that?*

CRAIG: *That was her fault.*

JESS: [Looking round] *What a dump!*

[Scott emerges from the garage in his overalls as Phil inspects the damage]

SCOTT: *Are you OK?*

PHIL: *Who's going to pay for this?*

MAGGIE: *Don't look at me.*

SCOTT: *Maybe you should calm down. Exchange names, addresses, insurance details.*

JESS: *There's no need. They know each other intimately.*

PHIL: *Jess!*

SCOTT: *I'm sorry?*

MAGGIE: *We're together. I'm Maggie. This is Phil. My er....*

PHIL: *Partner.*

SCOTT: *But you're travelling separately?*

MAGGIE: *We have our reasons.*

[Ashley, on his way to the shop, comes over. In B/G we see Nicola come out of the shop and take a look at the crash]

ASHLEY: *Anything I can do to help?*

LUCY: *I'm starving. Can't we just get there?*

ASHLEY: *Where are you going?*

▼ The judges (*left to right*) Yvon Grace, Bill Lyons, Paul de Freitas.

▲ Paul mingles with the crowd at an open audition.

▶
'WHO'S THE DADDY?'
Johnny Kinch feels
confident as he gets
through another stage.

▲ Jason Hain, not quite believing he's through to the semis.

◄ Nicola Orr.

▼ Jo-Ann D'Costa – she gave up the job offer of children's TV presenter to take part in *Soapstars*.

▲ Two early contestants, Andy White and
Maria Sophia Andreas, play 'Marlon' and
'Tricia' at the London open audition.

►
Ashra Price, looking
a little starstruck.

▼ Craig Henderson's improvised
scene – but will he get his kiss?

Emma Pollard and Dean Cook on the first day of the semi-finals.

▲ Brian McDevitt performing at his audition.

► Dee Whitehead.

Elspeth Brodie and Nicola Orr wait to be called.

▲ Erin Lordan in earlier days as a Hot Gossip dancer (*middle*).

► Erin Lordan.

▼ Ruth goes for the realistic face-slap ...

▲ ... and is shocked ...

►
... as she realises that
Debra's sporting a
real-life sore face!

▶ Erin Lordan and Brian McDevitt at the semis – they were finally to lose out as 'mum' and 'dad'.

▼ Yvon gives encouragement to Debra Michaels.

▲ Debra Michaels in a previous role as the Wicked Fairy Carabosse in 'Sleeping Beauty'.

▲ It's not hard to see why Dee Whitehead and Ashra Price were thought to be a potential mother/daughter combination in the early stages.

▲ Becky Weeks.

▲ Victoria Tonge. The intensity of the auditions is clear.

▲ Mark Jardine in his cabaret days.

▼ Together for the first time – eventual 'mum' and 'dad', Dee Whitehead and Mark Jardine at the first day of the semis.

▲ Elspeth and her lucky teddy wait for the judges to reach a decision.

◀ (*Left to right*) Dean Abrahams, Gemma Baker and Brian McDevitt rehearse a scene.

▼ Some of the finalists relieve the tension with a good neckrub.

◄ Patrick Tucker directs the hopefuls.

▲ The finalists watch Patrick's tuition ...

◄ ...and (*left to right*) Dean Cook, Debra Michaels, Ide Chiahmen and Dean Abrahams watch the playback of their scenes during the class.

▲ The 'deep three' in action – Craig Henderson,
Ruth Abram and Johnny Kinch.

▼ Tim Fee gives the hopefuls a
tour of Emmerdale village.

◀ Ruth calls her family –
she's through yet
another stage.

▼ Debra Michaels, Dee
Whitehead and Debbie
Dawson getting on famously.

◀ The hopefuls
leave Emmerdale
– but who will
be returning?

▲ The new family toast their success – (*left to right*) Elspeth, Ruth, Mark, Dee and Jason.

▶
Jason faces his first pile of scripts.

▼ Steve Frost and Keith Richardson meet the new 'family' at the safe house.

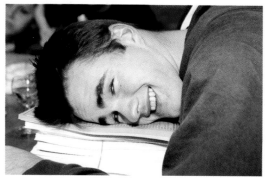

▶ Samantha Giles as *Emmerdale*'s Bernice Blackstock.

▼ Patrick Mower as Bernice's long-lost father, Rodney Blackstock. The contestants received the benefit of his experience first-hand during the auditions.

▲ The new family on
Blackpool Pier...

...and in their chalet in the ►
Emmerdale Holiday Village.

▼ Elspeth experiences her
first autograph signing.

▲ The first family portrait.

◀ And not forgetting the family dog: 'Dogstars' finalists, Sally and Bess.

PHIL: *The holiday village?*

LUCY: *We got lost.*

CRAIG: *No we didn't.*

MAGGIE: *Is it far?*

ASHLEY: *No, not at all.*

SCOTT: *Can I make a suggestion?*

JESS: *Like we turn around and go home?*

PHIL: *Not helpful.*

SCOTT: *Why don't you get a bite to eat in the pub? I'll look at your cars, then I'll take you there.*

PHIL: *Are you sure?*

SCOTT: *I've got to go there anyway.*

MAGGIE: *Thanks –*

SCOTT: *– Scott.*

MAGGIE: *Scott. That's really kind of you.*

SCOTT: *No problem.*

PHIL: *Come on, gang.*

[Phil and Maggie hand the car keys to Scott and Phil leads the way to the pub. Craig looks across appreciatively at Chloe and Charity, who emerge from the shop as Nicola goes back in. They walk towards Charity's cottage]

ASHLEY: *Your good deed for the day?*

SCOTT: *I'm going to charge them.*

For the judges as well as the actors, this is the first chance to see how well the hopefuls fit the characters the winners will be playing. There's not a vast amount to go on here. As with every script, there's plenty left open for an individual to interpret and bring to the role. It's interesting to see a hint as to how different people would play the same part, and it brings home how the judges haven't just been picking people who conform to one 'look' or 'style'. The judges also get groups up to see how they look together. They see Jo-Ann and Erin together, and are pleased. Outside, Jo-Ann's more optimistic – 'Erin's mum's half-Indian, and you can't really see it, but when you stand us next to each other, there's definitely something. That makes me feel better – I'm not an orphan!'

Johnny Kinch is worried he's not being called up. 'You can't help being a bit paranoid when everyone else is getting close ups and you're not'.

That afternoon, the judges and Steve and Keith convene to share their thoughts on what they've seen this morning. Before they start, Keith Richardson tells them, 'It's such a huge sense of relief. It's good to get into that room and feel the energy, I'm remarkably impressed by them.' Steve Frost agrees that he's encouraged. They go through each of the finalists in turn, checking their worksheets, which list the contenders in alphabetical order:

dean abrahams

KEITH: *I liked him – I've put a star down by his name.*

BILL: *I like him, I just think he's too young. He's a good actor.*

STEVE: *He's chirpy.*

BILL: *I'm just thinking of his life in the show. I wonder if some of the girls in the show would be interested in him. He's been more successful than the other Dean at playing it a little older.*

ruth abram

PAUL: *I'm a big fan.*

STEVE: *Her strength comes through. She's very self-composed.*

PAUL: *She's grown with the process, too. Each time we've seen her, she's grown stronger.*

KEITH: *I've put a big star against her. She's really good.*

gemma baker

STEVE: *She left me cold, I'm afraid.*

BILL: *In fairness, she's been much weaker today.*

KEITH: *I'm not getting any sense of strength.*

PAUL: *She's never blown me away as an actress. I think she's got a beautiful face. She looks fantastic on camera. Unlike Ruth, though, she's not grown with the process. She has potential, but she's not there yet, and we need it now.*

KEITH: *I've put 'not memorable'.*

YVON: *I think she's forgettable.*

elspeth brodie

BILL: *I loved her.*

KEITH: *She's very good. And a fellow Scot.*

dean cook

PAUL: *His acting is consistently good. Bill has reservations, though.*

BILL: *He's too young. He doesn't fit the brief.*

YVON: *He's cute incarnate, though.*

debbie dawson

YVON: *She's been a good performer, but wasn't today.*

PAUL: *She was disappointing today.*

STEVE: *I thought she was quite flat.*

PAUL: *She has been very good, she's only fallen down today.*

STEVE: *She's in a very strong field.*

BILL: *She was much better when she was just handed a script – it's almost as though preparing for it lets her down.*

STEVE: *Which could be a handy skill for an* Emmerdale *actress.*

jo-ann d'costa

PAUL: I really like her.

YVON: I've got a big question mark. I think she's affected.

KEITH: I've written 'slightly affected', and we were at opposite ends of the table, so I wasn't peeking.

BILL: I like her, too.

STEVE: I didn't find her affected as an actor. She's a bit of a performer, but she's going to be playing a sixteen-year-old girl who's a bit of a performer.

YVON: I like her.

PAUL: She responds well to direction. We can direct that out of her.

KEITH: Oh, I wouldn't rule her out, not at all.

YVON: I like her, but she's not my favourite.

ide chiahmen

BILL: No, not for me.

PAUL: We thought there was room for her to grow, but she hasn't really.

YVON: She's in a strong group, and she's not cutting it with the rest of them.

vicki greenwood

YVON: She's been my favourite since the beginning, but she's getting worse.

PAUL: Her voice is a bit flat, a bit monotone.

BILL: I liked her very much earlier on. She needs to work on her comedy. I find her performances a bit dour.

STEVE: She's good, but she needs a little more sparkle.

PAUL: I've said that from the start.

BILL: You did.

STEVE: She's very natural, she's got a lot of potential.

jason hain

YVON: He's grown on me. I had it in for him.

BILL: I like him.

STEVE: I can remember him from the first day of the semis, and there are only a few people there who stood out from the crowd. He stood out again today.

YVON: I thought he was too camp.

STEVE: Yeah, I remember, but he's brought that right down.

BILL: He's best on the light stuff, but he did well today with the abortion scene.

KEITH: [indicating worksheet] He's got a star.

craig henderson

STEVE: I've always really liked him. He's the only one who'd cause waves with the female cast. He'd be a rival for Scott.

KEITH: He's terribly quiet.

PAUL: For me it's the same as Vicki Greenwood – he needs sparkle. He's a good actor, he's consistent. But is he a star?

BILL: With some of the others we've seen development, but with him what you see is what you get. He's a developed actor. He'll bring that to the series, but he won't grow.

YVON: He's very aware of himself as an actor all the time.

BILL: You're saying he's a professional. He stands out as a professional.

YVON: I've got a question mark next to his name.

STEVE: Keeping him in gives us more options.

BILL: He's certainly not a risk. All the others are a risk, one way or another.

mark jardine

PAUL: He's really come on in leaps and bounds.

YVON: He's been an actor for fifteen years, which really surprised me, because he wasn't a performer of massive might at the beginning.

STEVE: *I was surprised and impressed by him. He was a lot better today than I remember.*

PAUL: *He was great in that* Cold Feet *scene at the semis. We'd made our mind up he was going, but –*

BILL: *The comedy scenes really sorted them out, you really saw the people that couldn't play them. He was just the opposite.*

YVON: *He's good, but he's not sexy enough.*

STEVE: *He fills a role in the show, he fits the brief. There's an attractive warmth, I think.*

PAUL: *Everyone's proved themselves, and this is all about that.*

STEVE: *He could play the dad. He's a believable dad.*

johnny kinch

YVON: *We've got stronger dads for our brief.*

PAUL: *His acting is consistent, but he doesn't fit the brief.*

BILL: *I've been saying all along he's an* EastEnders *actor. He's a good actor, I wouldn't scream if he was cast, but –*

PAUL: *I can see him on* London's Burning, The Bill. *He's London.*

KEITH: *I think he's good.*

PAUL: *He's likeable. He's castable.*

erin lordan

YVON: *A very* Emmerdale *look.*

BILL: *Well, yeah. She looks like Leah.*

STEVE: *She looks great. She's the sexy mum, if we want that. She's a bit stagy, but only a bit.*

BILL: *She's got much less stagy as it's gone on.*

YVON: *I've written 'weird facial thing'.*

BILL: *Oh, in that scene she just did? Yeah, I noticed that – it seemed such an odd choice to want to distort her looks like that. Beautiful woman... gurning. Why do that?*

PAUL: *It didn't bother me. She's really come on in leaps and bounds. She's so close.*

STEVE: *Oh, she's definitely still in the running.*

KEITH: *I've written 'good, but intense' and 'Quite sexy' which sounds more damning than I intended.*

paul mccarthy

YVON: *He's not a favourite of mine, and never has been.*

PAUL: *I like him. Again, he's a bit EastEnders, isn't he?*

BILL: *I think we've got at least two who are better. Possibly three.*

KEITH: *He's a little too young.*

brian mcdevitt

STEVE: I was a bit disappointed. From the tapes...

BILL: He's been my fave up until today.

KEITH: 'Scottish. Squeaks a little.'

STEVE: He was far and away the best until today.

PAUL: I think his nerves are getting to him. I think we should have a word.

debra michaels

YVON: She was lukewarm today.

BILL: I liked her before, she was awful today.

STEVE: I wouldn't say awful, but she wasn't particularly memorable.

PAUL: Keep her in, let's see what she comes up with.

YVON: It's the nerves again.

BILL: She's been so much better.

nicola orr

BILL: I don't think she was as good today as she's been.

KEITH: I thought she was good. I got a bit of a buzz, and that's been quite rare.

PAUL: She's got that spark, the one we were talking about. She's a good actress, too.

STEVE: I remember her from the semis, too.

YVON: She's young, but she's very grounded.

PAUL: But the problem is who her father would be. The only one who's been in the running is Paul, but I don't think he's going to be in the running much longer. She's terrific, though.

danielle pattinson

PAUL: I've let her go along, but they've really had to twist my arm.

YVON: She was good in the semis.

BILL: I thought she was good today in that miserable scene, she really seemed to understand it.

YVON: She doesn't engage with the scenes.

KEITH: She's so shy.

emma pollard

YVON: I've written 'No, no, no, whiny, whiny, whiny.' She looks good, her voice is so whiny.

PAUL: She's not won me over.

STEVE: 'No real understanding of lines.'

BILL: *She was good in the semis, she was good this morning.*

KEITH: *She's gorgeous, and she was good in that second scene today. But not good enough in this field.*

ashra price

YVON: *Ashra Price, who's been wearing that same red top all through this process, and probably has to have it surgically removed every night.*

BILL: *Perhaps she likes it.*

PAUL: *It's her lucky jumper. I do quite like her. I think we should keep her in the mix.*

BILL: *I do like her. She's pretty without being stick thin, and she can act. She's big and attractive, and that's healthy.*

STEVE: *She's very intelligent. Sharp.*

KEITH: *Is the age a problem?*

YVON: *I've been saying that all along. How old is she? I keep meaning to look it up. [Yvon reaches for Ashra's form] She's twenty-six! I said she was twenty-six, and you lot said she was twenty-two! I said she looked twenty-six. And she does, 'cos she is, so she doesn't fit the brief, so I was right all along!*

adrian russell

STEVE: *I just don't think so.*

PAUL: *He did get much better. He's not as strong as the others.*

BILL: *Looks good.*

STEVE: *He's charming, I think. Just not good, compared with the others.*

dee whitehead

YVON: *She's been the best today she's been so far.*

BILL: *I've always liked her, right from her first audition.*

KEITH: *I like her.*

STEVE: *She's really good.*

YVON: *And, you know, I think she could be a sexy mum, too.*

STEVE: *She's got a lot of life. She gives really intelligent readings of scenes.*

BILL: *There's this nagging doubt I have that goes 'a bit Howard's Way'. Old-fashioned.*

PAUL: *That's rich, coming from someone who played a Dalek in* Doctor Who [Purists would point out that Bill never played a Dalek, but was a guard in the 1967 Patrick Troughton serial *The Enemy of the World*]. *Only you remember* Howard's Way.

BILL: *She's really come up this week. Some of the others have gone down, She's gone up.*

YVON: *She's much more confident.*

becky weeks

YVON: *I like her, but I keep wavering.*

BILL: *She's in a really tough field.*

STEVE: *She's intelligent, professional. She's good, an appealing look.*

YVON: *I don't think she's that consistent.*

KEITH: *She looks a lot like a character we've got already. And there are a lot of good girls to choose from. She needs a little voice training, I think. Just a little.*

Once that's done, Steve Frost has to rush back to *Emmerdale* to a story conference, but he's relatively happy: 'It proves to me that the process has worked, I think, because clearly of the twenty-four people we've seen today, you can see why they're here, they've all got some kind of ability. It seemed haphazard, but I'm encouraged we'll get five people that can act, that can be a family and that fulfil the brief.'

Once every three weeks, all the *Emmerdale* writers meet up with the producer, storyliners and script editors to discuss the next block of scripts and the future direction of the stories and characters. Although it's not even September yet, they'll be discussing the Christmas and New Year episodes today – a traditional time for big stories as the soaps try to win the Christmas ratings war. There will be the usual mix of births, marriages and deaths on the agenda. Christmas will also be two months into the initial three-month contracts for the new family. Before they even start their job, the storylines will be in place for their whole initial contract period.

That's not to say that they are guaranteed an extension – scripts can be changed, characters can be written out or downplayed if they aren't working. It's certainly not unusual to have storylines and scripts written well before the actors have been cast. Often, for a relatively small part, the casting will be done only a few days before filming. For a regular role, an actor would be contracted only a few weeks before they started work. Scripts are not written around an actor at first. Obviously, once the writers have seen an actor in action, and seen where their strengths lie, and which other characters they have screen chemistry with, the scripts can be tailored to a specific performance.

In this case, the actors are really starting to get to know each other. It could prove an advantage later – the shared experience of the *Soapstars* auditions might make them bond as a family on screen. The judges aren't going to pick actors on how well they get on with each other, but they've noticed that Jason and Dee are popular with the others.

Bill Lyons would normally be at the story conference, but he doesn't seem devastated to be skipping it. He's continuing to write for *Emmerdale* while he's working on *Soapstars*. He's got his latest script, written in longhand, in his bag. Bill's proud of his Luddite reputation – he reckons his having a teletext TV is pushing it. He's one of two writers with special dispensation from YTV to supply their scripts typed, rather than word processed, the other one being Alan Plater. By now he's written a few scripts for the new family. His favourite character is Jess, the elder daughter, but he's not found himself picturing any particular actress in the role – there are a number of them that could do the job. He admits he's got his favourites by now, but won't say who they are.

While the judges deliberate, the finalists meet Patrick Tucker, a director, whose soap credential is that he's a regular director on *Brookside*. Patrick is the author of the book *Secrets of Screen Acting*. This is one of the most highly regarded books on the subject, and one popular in America amongst the actors and drama coaches who eschew 'method acting', which is still the orthodoxy in most acting classes and workshops on the other side of the Atlantic. Patrick is a champion of the more pragmatic British school of acting, his talk is full of anecdotes about how the best British actors bring a series of techniques and 'cheats' to best interpret the script; they don't feel the need to spend three months working as taxi drivers or in mental asylums to understand their part.

Patrick's maxim is: the truth is what the screen says, not what you feel. To illustrate his point, Patrick gets Johnny Kinch up in front of a camera, then asks him to adopt a neutral expression, empty his mind of any feelings. Then, he asks Johnny simply turn his head to face the camera, swallow, then open his mouth. The finalists watch the playback of Johnny doing just this. Patrick gives the image on the monitor a line to react to. When Johnny's told his mother is ill, he gives a shocked reaction. When he's told he's won the Lottery, he reacts with bemused delight. When he's told his wife is pregnant, the expression of joy is unmistakable. It is, of course, the same piece of footage every time. Patrick wants to get across the point that it's what the camera sees that's important with television acting, not what the actor feels.

Patrick asks the auditionees to line up, then sit down one at a time, face camera right then do something of their own choosing to camera for fifteen seconds. He turns up the pressure a little, starts to shout, gets them to hurry along. It's another trick, of course, and almost all the finalists fall for it. A couple of them, hearing the phrase 'fifteen seconds' simply repeat the performance that got them noticed in the open auditions. A couple try tongue twisters, or a joke. Craig Henderson impersonates Yoda, to much acclaim. But with the notable exception of Becky Weeks, who sits silently, doing small reactions, the vast majority gabble, most still project out to the crowd. Most sit quite rigidly. Almost all of them face camera *left*.

It's all exactly what Patrick expected them to do. He does a quick run-through – only a couple of them used more than about a twelfth of the screen during their performance. Patrick brandishes a spatula, slapping it against the monitor. He starts hurrying them along – and you can see the finalists getting progressively more animated. He stresses that the mood of the director should never affect a performance. They only had fifteen seconds in front of a camera – but that doesn't mean they couldn't take a second or two before that to compose themselves. On a programme like *Emmerdale*, where a director has to get eight or nine scenes recorded before breaking for lunch, he or she will start to get agitated as the morning moves on. But the cast can't afford to be, not if the script demands them to be reflective, romantic or relaxed. And, for heaven's sake, if you don't know which one is 'camera right', then *ask*. As the cast move around the studio during shots, directions like 'left' and 'right' are pretty meaningless. The camera is the nearest thing there is to a fixed point, and 'camera right', say, is to the right of the cameraman *from the cameraman's point of view.*

The finalists watch the playbacks, most of them realizing they've still got a lot to learn. Perhaps surprisingly, this is the first time the finalists have seen themselves on screen during the *Soapstars* process. While Tim and his crew have shot many hundreds of hours of material, and the judges have mainly been watching the hopefuls via their monitor since early on, the hopefuls have not seen any of that. For some, like Dean Cook and Gemma Baker, seeing themselves on television is something they are used to. But there are still a few, like Nicola Orr and Vicki Greenwood, who've never seen themselves on screen except for the odd wedding or christening on a family camcorder. 'I didn't think I looked like that,' Nicola confesses, 'you picture yourself different. But that's the reality, that's how I look.'

Most of the others have some screen experience, but it's still a relative novelty. It's also a chance to see how people look and sound on screen, rather than in the flesh. It changes some people's opinions – Mark Jardine's, for example: 'I always saw Johnny Kinch as my main rival, until I watched the playbacks with Patrick Tucker. Brian was very quiet and, sitting in the audience, it wasn't always possible to hear him, but that's because he was acting for the camera. Brian was really good on screen. That's what the panel were judging us on, of course.'

There are some basic pieces of etiquette that Patrick runs through – the most fundamental being that it's up to the director to shout 'cut'. Actors should keep going until told otherwise, however disastrously the scene seems to be going.

Then Patrick illustrates some tricks of the trade. It's important to keep as much of your face in shot as you can. It's common in a soap for two people to argue while one, usually the shortest, has their back to the other. In real life, people don't have arguments like that. It works on the screen for a number of reasons – first, it allows the audience to see both faces in one shot. More subtly, it allows both actors to show what they are thinking. If they aren't face-to-face, a character's face can contradict the words they're saying. They can plead with a character to forgive them, while their expression shows that they're being manipulative or secretly pleased. If the characters faced each other, the audience would wonder why their victim was being so stupid that they didn't notice the expression on the face in front of them.

These 'cheated eyelines' are a common part of the grammar of telling a story in TV drama – but the actors need to motivate them, they need to come up with a reason why their character is looking away. If you play close attention to the way a lot of soap scenes are blocked out, people are just not standing where they would in relation to each other in the real world in the same situation. We don't notice because, as Patrick says, it's not reality, it's the appearance of reality that's important.

Patrick tells the finalists to use more of the screen – if they are going to use their hands, or hold something, then they might have to do so at what, in the real world, would be an odd angle. Hands should be completely in shot, or completely out of shot – and in a close-up, to see an actor's hands, they'd have to hold them level with their head. 'The truth is not your friend,' he says – the actors have to be convincing, but that's not the same as being naturalistic. Camera angles and cheated eyelines mean that people in the same scene are often really standing in ridiculous positions in relation to each other, but it all works on camera.

There are some useful hints and tips – react before speaking. It's not the natural thing to do, but it makes it easier for an audience to understand what a character is feeling, as well as making it harder for an editor to edit out their performance. The camera will pick up slow movements better than fast ones – so take your time getting up out of a chair, or picking up a cup.

The most useful advice at this point, for a group of actors mostly more used to stage work, is about the level of their voices. Because they're in an audition hall, the finalists have all been projecting their voices a little. Patrick tells them to project only as far as the microphone boom. This can mean that the other person in the scene has difficulty hearing – but it will work for the specific shot they are in. He also warns them that it's a very common failing to speak slowly when speaking softly.

Patrick sends them away for the night with one of three scripts to learn. The finalists are in buoyant mood – they've been given a lot to think about. At the same time, they know that tomorrow is going to be crucial.

day two

The finalists had a good time in the hotel the previous night. Some of them are nursing hangovers. Even those that got an early night didn't get much sleep. There was a balance – people wanted to relax, they wanted to socialize with the other finalists – but as Craig says, there's a 'conflict of interest': they don't want to blow their chances because they were up drinking until two in the morning. The pressure is getting to most of the finalists. Erin Lordan: 'This is the most intense part of the process, we're learning so much about TV technique, at the same time the stakes are so high now that you're conscious of every fluffed word. So it means some real highs and lows.' They cope in different ways – some, like Johnny Kinch, become more extrovert, and start pacing around, making jokes. At some point during the week, most people find a corner to go off to have a little cry, or just some peace from the camera crews when the pressure gets to them. Jason alarms a few people by sitting in a corner, singing to himself at one point. The only exception is Vicki Greenwood, who seems to take perverse pleasure in pressure, and spends most of the tense moments grinning. Everyone's in the same boat, and there's a lot of hugging and support.

The finalists all agree that it's the waiting that gets to them. Even with a 'fly on the wall' show like *Soapstars*, it takes time to set up lighting, to rig microphones and to plan the best way to achieve shots. It means that between each segment of the process there's a 'twenty-minute break', which can often stretch to almost an hour. It's nice and sunny, so the finalists sit just outside, under a tree, sunbathing, reading magazines, dozing, chatting. There's a general consensus that the best day so far was the second day of the semi-finals, when they had the most to do, and they were thrown the script they had to learn in half an hour. It kept them on their toes.

Today, it quickly transpires, will be another day like that. Patrick Tucker has returned, spatula at the ready, and tells them that what he's doing today will be close to a typical soap schedule. There are eight scenes to shoot, family scenes from *Emmerdale* with everyone taking turns to be involved. Patrick's been told to have the eight scenes ready for the judges when they arrive at lunchtime, and they've started a little after nine.

The finalists have been learning individual scenes ever since stage two of the open auditions. This is the most sophisticated variation on that so far, though – it's taken for granted that everyone can learn their lines at this stage (and everyone is indeed word perfect). This will be a properly directed scene – the actors will have to hit their marks, and they'll have to think ahead to make sure they're in the right place to do that. It's a fully blocked-out scene.

Patrick has a particularly ambitious plan for one of the scenes. It starts with the family (minus the dad) sitting around the breakfast table, the dad of the family coming in, sitting down, confessing to an affair, then the daughters storming off while the mum listens in horror to the revelation. The son is in the background. It sounds straightforward enough, but actually requires a fair amount of choreography to work on camera. They have to plan exactly when everything happens, which direction the actors enter from and exit to. All five people sitting around the table have to have at least most of their face to camera – while making it look like a normal breakfast. Patrick tells Jo-Ann a good cheat – she's got to say she saw 'dad' with Tara at the stud. Regardless of the 'real' direction of the stud, if she turns to look in the rough direction of the camera, indicating the stud is 'over there', then the audience won't just see the back of her head, they'll see her expression. As people storm off, they have to carefully leave their chairs in the right place, so no one bumps into them later in the scene. 'Mum' has to get up and stand on the other side of the room – but in a natural way, without drawing attention to the fact that it's an actress doing it – so there can be a nice two-shot of just her and 'dad', a few seconds down the line. The scene ends with a 'deep three' – a close up of the mum, the dad in the middle distance and the son at back, his head appearing – if all goes to plan – between them. To help the actors, 'marks' are placed on the floor – little bits of gaffer tape. But, of course, they can't look down at the marks, they have to know where they are. They have to know where the camera is at all times without, of course, ever looking for it. And certainly not at it.

The actors know their lines, but now they have to memorize their marks, they have to relate that to the lines in the scene... and they have to act the scene in the most emotionally involving way. It's quite a challenge. This will be one continuous take, on one camera. If anyone messes up, they'll all have to start again from the top of the scene.

Patrick warns them that, on a soap, directors have very little time to dedicate to actors. There's a lot of demand on time as it is – the director will spend most of it with the cameramen, the sound men, the lighting engineers, making sure that his shot works technically. In the end, if the actors put in an award-winning performance but it's shot in a way that isn't usable in the programme, then it won't get shown. It's a fact of life that an adequate performance that they can use will get screened rather than a great one the camera doesn't capture. Patrick's notes to the actors are mostly to do with hitting their marks. His character notes are so vague as to be almost useless – 'more angry', 'make more of that moment'. He jokes that one of his colleagues, when asked by an actor for guidance, invariably says 'more intense', regardless of the circumstances, and that the actor tends to go away happy.

They're working to a strict deadline this morning – again, demanding schedules are a fact of life on any soap, especially one that's on five nights a week, such as

Emmerdale. They have time for a run-through (what, on *Emmerdale*, would be called a 'camera rehearsal'), then it's straight into recording the finished scene.

Patrick doesn't really need to pile on the pressure – there's a lot to get through. On the whole, the finalists do very well. Johnny Kinch gets a couple of goes, because one of the scenes is short a dad, and even manages to improvise a little bit by sniffing a bunch of flowers, which gets a laugh – it's exactly the sort of 'adding to a scene' that Bill's been looking for from the beginning. Despite the nerves, and the knowledge that a third of the auditionees will be eliminated by the end of the day, everyone's at the top of their game.

They finish only slightly behind schedule, and the judges are brought in.

Paul has spent the morning answering letters. A few of the semi-finalists who didn't make it to the finals have written to him, thanking him for seeing them and asking for advice how to take it further. Paul's taking time to reply to them all, and finds it gratifying that people's experiences on *Soapstars* are helping them to get a little further in the industry. He jots some notes for Victoria Tonge, before being called back into the audition hall.

The finalists take turns to sit on the front row and watch the playbacks. The judges are also watching. This is the most important performance of the week, seeing the finalists performing as a family, on screen, in a scene they've not had long to learn. It's easily the closest they've had yet to doing the job they will have to if they're picked. They watch the screen intently during the playback, not a single one of them so much as glances at the judges. At the end of each scene, the finalists applaud. Everyone's done well.

The judges watch the playbacks with a little less enthusiasm – they were hoping for a little more acting coaching, and less of the fancy camera angles. Bill's sure they've had a 'deep three' on *Emmerdale*, but can't for the life of him remember when – 'We tend to use actors, not effing chess pieces,' he notes sagely, moderating his language. Bill's also annoyed that Patrick's changed the scenes – in one case, the 'dads' are playing lines written for Angie. 'Call me old-fashioned, but I want to see blokes playing parts written for blokes. This isn't giving them the best chance to play the parts. This is unfair on them.'

Patrick goes back over to the finalists and tells them that it's OK to change lines if they feel their character wouldn't say them. It's difficult to work out whether it's writer Bill or producer Yvon who's the most shocked. There are a number of serious objections – as a writer, Bill's not thrilled with the idea of people changing his work, and points out that by the time it reaches the actors, the script has been checked, amended and altered for several weeks, with almost a dozen people directly part of that process. The story is discussed at story conference. One of the storyliners writes the storyline; the story editor approves it; the producer and storyliners spend a whole day going over every line; the storyline is amended; the producer approves it. All the writers pore over the scripts at the next story conference; a writer writes the script; the script editor edits it; the writer rewrites it; when the script editor approves it, they pass it to the producer, who also approves it. Then it's sent to the director, who may also suggest alterations to the writer and script editor. If an actor wants to change a line, they had better have a very good reason for wanting to, and they'd better seek approval from the script editor first, via the director. It's not something that's done lightly.

Yvon's aware of that, and is also concerned with practicalities – start changing words, and other actors might start missing their cues. On a set, actors might start moving into position when they hear another actor say a certain word. If that word doesn't come, neither will the actor. More than that – there are often nuances to what's said that an actor might not appreciate, because they aren't always aware of the bigger picture. They might be saying their line to put an ironic spin on something that was said in an early scene, or the writer might have them say something that hints at a future storyline that they are unaware of. Established actors do have some leeway – because they know their character, they might pick up on a continuity point. If faced with a line like, 'I don't have any brothers or sisters', they might remember that five years ago there was mention of a sister. They also talk to the producer, from time to time, about the direction of their character. But all but the most minor change to a script on the studio floor is a big no-no.

The finalists like Patrick, though, and think his advice has been really useful. Some, like Brian, have reservations about his 'sweetie, darling' manner, but they've all had a useful day getting acting coaching – it's a course they'd usually have to pay to go on.

Debra Michaels says it's 'brilliant, something you can take away with you'. Dee agrees: 'he's making it really fun'. Debbie Dawson is keen to put what she's learned into action. Jason Hain's also impressed: 'I did some TV stuff at Uni, and it wasn't as in-depth as what he was telling us just now'.

Afterwards, Patrick says he's impressed by the general standard, but feels that far too many of the finalists are still too stagy. His credo is that screen acting is almost a completely different discipline to stage acting, and that a lot of the things that work well on stage are the exact opposite of what works on screen. 'In the theatre you push *out* to the audience; on screen you pull the audience *in*.' Those with stage experience have a lot to unlearn.

Here, at least, Bill agrees with Patrick. 'It's the general thing when you first get actors on the soap: they give much bigger performances than they need to,' he says. 'If you look at acting as a talent and you go from stage on the one end of the scale to film on the other, a stage actor has a performance of a certain size because you have to, 'cos you're reaching an audience…. you look at a film actor on the other end – when they raise an eyebrow it becomes quite a large movement, which you wouldn't see on stage. And television and soap is sort of in the middle. I mean, straight acting on television is probably marginally more subtle, I would confess, than soap acting, but soap acting is still a relatively subtle mode… people think that it's something that you just pick up, but it isn't.

'If you look in *Emmerdale* at Peter Amory who plays Chris, considering at times the character is just an extreme villain, he plays a lot of things with a wry humour, he plays against it. Because we do things at such a rate, you require an actor to think, "Do I play this the obvious way or is there something else that I get out of it?" and that comes from the actor. In a way it can't come from us entirely, because you're knocking out these things at a rate of knots….

'With shouty scenes, there are ways where you can have an argument and someone is gonna look at the same lines and one person will spend his whole time throughout the scene shouting at the other person. The other person can use a bit of sarcasm, a bit of humour, so that the line seems to be funny and you don't get the kick in the tail until afterwards. Well, that's good acting. I mean, it's looking at what you've got there and varying what you're doing within the part. Those are the people that last really, the people that can find something in whatever they do.'

The hopefuls have always been aware of the cameras; they've understood that the *Soapstars* crew are filming them and their reactions. After Patrick, though, they seem more conscious of the DV crews wandering around. Patrick told them that the camera lens ought to be a magnet for their faces. A number of the finalists are now far more interested in how they are coming across. Most of them are now glancing up to check where the cameras are before doing anything. The presence of the *Emmerdale* producers has driven home how close they now are to getting the parts. It's a tense time for all.

That afternoon, the judges have some serious work to do – whittling down the twenty-four finalists to fifteen. It'll take a while, and so they leave the finalists in the capable hands of Tim Fee, the line producer of *Emmerdale*.

Tim Fee has been line producer since 1988 (although until last year his official title was 'production controller'). Over the years, he's become an ambassador for *Emmerdale*, he's shown network executives and other special guests around the village set, he's championed the programme,

BILL LYONS, panellist

'Whatever way you look at it, this is a factory situation. Two hundred and sixty episodes a year; not every one is gonna be Kafka.'

> TIM FEE, *Emmerdale*'s line producer
>
> 'If you're successful, you'll become popular people. But if you approach the job without utter discipline, you won't survive'.

and is extremely proud of the BAFTA award earlier this year. His enthusiasm for the show is infectious.

Today, though, he's here to break some of the realities of the production of *Emmerdale* to the finalists. Making ten episodes a fortnight, fifty weeks a year, is quite a task. The successful *Soapstars* will have their work cut out – each script is about seventy-five pages long, and every two weeks, they'll be sent ten scripts to learn. Seven hundred and fifty pages of scripts. Obviously they won't be in every scene, so won't have to learn every line, but they will be in a substantial number of scenes, and they'll need to know what's happening in the rest of the episode. The actors are sent scripts a fortnight before recording, and no one will be testing their knowledge or helping them out – it'll be up to them to know their scenes inside out by the time they get to the studio.

Once they actually get on the programme, of course, they'll also have to contend with the episodes currently in production. Tim stresses that *Emmerdale* has a reputation for having the friendliest cast and crew in the industry – but they aren't people who forgive unprofessional behaviour. It's a team, and if one part of that team isn't pulling their weight, everyone suffers. Friendliness isn't going to stop the producer from making hard-nosed decisions.

Despite the tension, there's genuine excitement in the air. All but the most pessimistic finalists have started to contemplate the possibility of working on the show by now.

Tim Fee explains the sort of life they can expect – a working day that often runs from half-seven in the morning to half-seven in the evening. Wake-up call is at half-five, the women going in even earlier to get their make-up done. You get the weekends off, except in special circumstances. You can book holidays – as long as you put your application in to the producer at least a few months in advance. In the past, they have needed actors to cancel a holiday because of an important storyline once or twice. In an emergency, you can get the morning off – a couple of years ago Freya Copeland, who plays Angie, broke her wrist in several places while mountain biking on a Sunday afternoon. They rescheduled her scenes so that she wasn't required back until Tuesday.

One question on everybody's lips is... what about the money? Tim smiles – it's not big money. They're paid per episode they appear in, and they'll be surprised how little they get per episode (although with 250-plus episodes a year, he admits it can add up). They'll become well known, famous even, but there's no guarantee that will translate into a stellar career once they leave. If they go on to bigger and better things, they'll be the exception, rather than the rule. *Emmerdale*'s always in the top five programmes – in fact, it's usually in the top three. It's usually downhill from here. The lucky people who go on to work on *Emmerdale* will be seen by the public as the characters, not as themselves. They're condemned, at least until they're completely forgotten about, to have people coming up to them in the street to ask where their fictional husband or wife is, or to do a terrible impersonation of them.

It's around this time that the finalists stop talking about 'winning' the part.

emmerdale at last

CHAPTER SIX

Wednesday 29 August, 2001. Day two of the finals and the finalists visit the Emmerdale *set, while the judges decide which fifteen are to make it through to the next stage.*

Emmerdale is a real place. Don't let anyone tell you anything different.

The village doesn't appear on any maps, but it sits in a notoriously windy part of the Yorkshire countryside. There are over a dozen buildings, including a village hall and Post Office, and the famous Woolpack pub. The river Emm flows under a stone road bridge, then on past the cricket field. The village is surrounded by isolated cottages, farms and barns. An English heritage sign notes the places of historical interest, though there are few visitors, only people there on business. But those that are lucky enough to go are all agreed – it looks just like a real village.

It is, of course, the purpose-built outdoor set where the village location scenes of *Emmerdale* are recorded. It's thought to be the largest permanent set built for a television programme anywhere in the world, and was designed to be filmed from any angle. It's lavish compared with its competitors – Albert Square is actually much smaller than it looks, and a few of the 'buildings' are actually just facades. Turn the corner of Coronation Street and you end up in the Baker Street of the Granada *Sherlock Holmes* series. Emmerdale village isn't an illusion; it's a real place.

A number of interiors are based out at the village set, such as the Reynolds' house and the vet's surgery, but for the most part the inside scenes are recorded back at the *Emmerdale* studio in the middle of Leeds. Even here, there's a lot to be impressed by. At 26,000 square feet, the studio is the largest single stage in Europe. But walking around, you're struck by the attention to detail, much of which just isn't visible on screen. The camera never gets close enough to read the timetable at the bus stop, or the menus in Marlon's restaurant, but the designers have filled them out. You could plan your journey from Emmerdale to Hotten or Leeds, you could work out how much change you'd get for a tenner if you ordered the lemon chicken at the Woolpack.

When Tim tells our budding soap stars that the time has come to take them to Emmerdale village, the excitement is palpable. They'll be impressed, he tells them. But he's taking them on a beautiful August afternoon – this is as good as the weather's going to get. 'There's a Yorkshire expression,' Tim tells them, '"It's the last place God made".' It's very picturesque, but it can also get very cold, and it's always fairly windy. As *Emmerdale*'s recorded six to eight weeks before it's shown, any scenes with characters sunbathing in June are recorded in April.

It's a fifteen-minute trip by coach. Unsurprisingly, the finalists spend the time mulling over Tim's pep talk, and are preoccupied with the judges' impending decision. The finalists genuinely aren't sure whether they are through, even after the weeks of hard slog and uncertainty that they've been through to get this far. A fair few aren't sure now if it's a prize worth winning, but most knew what they were letting

JASON HAIN, finalist

'This is bizarre, this is fab, wicked. My God, I could be working here in a couple of months.'

themselves in for. Tim's talk has been a stark reminder, though, that it's not over when the judges announce who's got the parts – it's just the beginning. For the vast majority, getting the part would still be a dream; they are still keen to think they are in with a chance. That said, Emma Pollard seems more excited by the news that they're all going to Pizza Express for their meal that evening....

To get to the village set, the coach passes through some beautiful parts of the Yorkshire countryside. Unsurprisingly, some of the finalists are starting to talk about what they would do if they got the part. A few of the mums can really see themselves living here. Johnny Kinch has his heart set on a vintage Jaguar. No one's counting their chickens, yet, though.

Arriving at the site, everyone is required to get off the coach and walk through a disinfectant mat as a foot-and-mouth precaution. This event separates the townies from the people that live in the country, and is the first experience many of the Londoners have had of the crisis. Debra's worried about her slinky red shoes, and is confused – is the Emmerdale site really infected with foot-and-mouth? Tim Fee helpfully explains – there have been outbreaks just a few miles away, and this disinfectant will help *prevent* it from spreading there. And she's not to worry, her shoes will be fine.

The foot-and-mouth crisis has affected *Emmerdale*, and the production team have been happy to comply with a number of restrictions. Meanwhile, because the episodes are filmed weeks in advance, the storyliners have been wary of introducing a full-scale foot-and-mouth story. There have been several references to the crisis in the show, but Jack Sugden's farm has remained mercifully unaffected. Karen Grimes, one of *Emmerdale*'s two script editors, explains why:

'We obviously talked about a foot-and-mouth story, but there were all kinds of problems. First, we storyline months ahead. Even if we went back and inserted a foot-and-mouth story, it would be recorded five or six weeks ahead. We didn't know how long the outbreak would last – what might seem topical when it was written might have looked ridiculously out of date by the time it was shown. We were right in the middle of a story about Jack's herd getting TB, so we didn't want to go straight to another story just like it. We managed to put lines about the outbreak into existing scenes, and it's been in the background of the show for months now. But the main reason was entirely practical – the movement restrictions in place meant we couldn't have Batley the dog at the village site, let alone farm animals. So we'd have to have run a story about foot and mouth without seeing any cattle.'

The village is set back a mile or two from the road. The coach works its way round the narrow road to Emmerdale. The finalists catch sight of it to their left, in the distance.

The village is impressive, but it's not just a set – they are real buildings. Many are exact replicas of the original buildings used in the show when it was filmed on location, before the move to the village set. The village was built a little under four years ago. Since *Emmerdale* started, in 1972, the outside scenes had been filmed on location in the Yorkshire Dales – latterly in the beautiful village of Esholt. But this caused all sorts of problems. A lot of the people in Esholt benefited from the connection to *Emmerdale* – tourists flock there, the owner of the 'real' Woolpack gets a good trade from fans of the show. But just as many villagers were inconvenienced by the roads being closed and the crowds of production people, as well as tourists, all trying to park their cars.

It wasn't ideal for the people making *Emmerdale*, either – crowds of tourists gathered to watch the filming, and if one of them wandered into shot, took a photograph or even commented too loudly, filming would have to restart. Making television is an expensive business – for every actor in front of the camera, there are a dozen people standing behind it – cameramen, the director, the PAs, the runners, the make-up and costuming people, the soundmen, the lighting engineers, the drivers, the special effects men, the publicity people, the caterers. And that's just on the set; there are far more people working on the programme. Time is money.

The switch to a purpose-built set was Tim Fee's idea. For a number of years, he'd calculated that building a multi-million pound set would actually save money, because it would be a private, controlled environment. More scenes could be recorded, faster. YTV were reluctant at first to invest the money, but once *Emmerdale* switched to three episodes a week, it became inevitable. It just wouldn't be possible to film enough scenes on location. A site was leased, and the bare fields were transformed into a village in eighteen weeks. The attention to detail is extraordinary – weeds were planted, ruts in driveways were carefully set out, there are even patches of discoloured tarmac, suggesting old roadworks. The buildings were aged using agricultural slurry – at least until health and safety found out.

Back in the Blue Room, Yvon's pleased the finalists have got the chance to go to the village: 'It's fab. It's such a brilliant world to be part of. There's nothing more exciting than working in television. I mean that's why I do it…. Whether you're behind the camera, in front of the camera, it doesn't matter because the pace is always really exciting, the people are great, you're working with really exciting technicians and creative people… there's always a buzz. When you walk on a set, even when the set's empty, actually – when I used to do *EastEnders*, when I was a baby script editor – I'd go onto the set when it was all empty and go, "Ooh fab, Dot Cotton's cupboard." It's just exciting. I can't explain it, it's like… theatre distilled. It's an intense version of theatre.'

Jason Hain's even more enthusiastic. He watches *Emmerdale*, his mum loves it, and he keeps handing his camera to members of the production team to get his picture taken alongside all the landmarks.

Not everyone's in such a sunny mood. A few of the younger finalists sit on the Butch Dingle memorial bench, unhappy – they reckon it's cruel to bring them all here when they probably already know which ten of them won't be here tomorrow.

Ashra's keen to see the *Soapstars* process end, so that the winners can get down to work.

The others are happier to be here. Tim Fee shows them around – many of the buildings are empty inside. The finalists are particularly disappointed to find that the Woolpack is bare. Next door, though, are the cottages that double up as the dressing rooms and green room for the actors. It's not exactly lavish, but it's comfortable enough. There are interiors that are used in the series. In the series, one of them used to be owned by Laura Johnstone, the Scottish lawyer.

The downstairs is just as Laura left it – complete with her certificates on the wall. Ashra and Jo-Ann have a good look round, and agree it would be a nice place to live, although the kitchen's a bit small. Dee and Debbie agree 'we could live here, it's beautiful'. For Dee 'it's becoming more real, I can imagine working here, now'.

Upstairs has been set up to be the Sugden bedrooms – the room Robert and Andy share, complete with football and Britney posters, Jack Sugden's bedroom, and little Victoria's room. Jo-Ann remembers seeing the room in the show a couple of nights ago. But these don't look like sets at all – they all look like real rooms.

The vet's surgery has a rather macabre secret – three stuffed rabbits and a stuffed dog sit in their cages. At first, a couple of the finalists don't realize they are stuffed. Erin is faced with an omen – one of the rabbits is called Erin, too. Does the presence of four rabbit feet make this a particularly good sign? No one's really sure.

The last stop is the graveyard. Tim gives them a tour – many of the tombstones are reclaimed from an 18th-century London site that was redeveloped, but there are newer stones here, too – Victor Windsor, Francis 'Butch' Dingle, Rachel Hughes, Frank Tate. Emmerdale has something of a reputation for being a dangerous place to live – there have been plenty of violent deaths and tragic accidents in recent years (although the makers insist that the death rates are no higher than in the other soaps). 'There's plenty of room for more,' Tim warns the finalists, gleefully.

The tour has taken about an hour. Now it's over, and the finalists start to head back to Trinity, to find out which fifteen of them are going through… and which nine are going home.

They don't have long to wait. The fifteen winners are called inside, one by one. There's more than a degree of fatalism about matters at this point. Vicki Greenwood and Erin Lordan are convinced they are out. Most people really aren't sure. A couple of them are quietly confident. The maths is simple – there are three candidates for each part. So, if you're a potential 'dad', and two other 'dads' have already been called – the odds are three to one against you. As more and more people get called, the patterns start to emerge, the odds lengthen on being called in.

Soon, nine people remain outside. In the end, the judges and *Emmerdale* producers have been pretty well in agreement who isn't going to make it:

DEAN COOK
'Very talented, terrific, too young' is Paul's verdict. Keith agrees – 'he's only going because of his age.' Yvon loves his face.

DEBBIE DAWSON
'Very natural, but not right for this part,' says Yvon.

IDE CHIAHMEN
'Needs to work at it, but there's a lot to look forward to' according to Paul. Keith reckons she was very good that morning, but agrees with Yvon that she's been overshadowed by others.

VICKI GREENWOOD
Bill thinks she's 'dour, and we're disappointed she didn't prove us wrong'. Paul thinks she's a good actress, and is disappointed she's going.

PAUL McCARTHY

Paul reckons he's 'talented, but too young and in a strong field'.

DANIELLE PATTINSON

'She had a lot to prove,' Yvon asserts, 'but she's not been on the same planet as everyone else today.'

EMMA POLLARD

'Gorgeous, has potential, but too much work needed,' is Paul's verdict. Bill agrees she should go, but says she's got 'A real perky quality, before long, with a bit more coaching and experience, she's going to get all sorts of offers.'

ASHRA PRICE

'I always had my doubts about her age,' Yvon says, surprising no one. Bill still likes her. Paul thinks she's been 'consistently good', but has been persuaded she's off-brief by Yvon. He thinks he can get her work elsewhere.

ADRIAN RUSSELL

'One hurdle behind what we need now,' says Paul. 'He's come on, though.'

The only question mark was Becky Weeks. Keith Richardson had been worried about her voice, but having seen more of her, he's been convinced she should progress.

They've all done extremely well to get this far, they've all benefited from the experience and contacts they've made... but they won't be here tomorrow. It's clear to everyone that some really talented people haven't made it.

Ashra has finally fallen foul of Yvon, who's persuaded

the others that she is too old to play a teenage daughter. Ashra's naturally upset – 'It's horrible to be rejected in the first round, but it's much worse at this stage, when you're so close.'

The last fifteen, then, are:

- ☐ Debra Michaels
- ☐ Dee Whitehead
- ☐ Erin Lordan
- ☐ Johnny Kinch
- ☐ Mark Jardine
- ☐ Brian McDevitt
- ☐ Ruth Abram
- ☐ Jo-Ann D'Costa
- ☐ Elspeth Brodie
- ☐ Becky Weeks
- ☐ Gemma Baker
- ☐ Nicola Orr
- ☐ Dean Abrahams
- ☐ Jason Hain
- ☐ Craig Henderson

The adult audition has clearly paid off – of the six adults remaining, four of them (all three mums and Mark Jardine) came from that last audition.

The remaining finalists are, predictably by now, given a new script to learn overnight. The judges promise that tomorrow won't be too intensive – everyone has to perform just one more scene. For some of the finalists, that sounds rather ominous... it's nearly the end of the road. Tomorrow, five more people will be dropped, and the judges will be left with straight alternatives for each role.

it can change your life

CHAPTER SEVEN

Getting a part in a series like Emmerdale *can change your life. But what sort of new life can the winning soap stars expect? The papers are full of pictures of soap actors at glitzy nightclubs or on foreign beaches, and stories about million-pound contracts, pop-star lovers and backroom bust-ups. Is it really like that? The best way to find out is to ask an actor on* Emmerdale.

profile 1: samantha giles

During the summer of 1998, Samantha Giles was a struggling actor with a few stage and TV credits and one film part on her CV. She persevered with her acting ambitions, but to support herself she had a day job working in Habitat. She went up to *Emmerdale* to audition for the part of Tricia Stokes. She didn't get it, but so impressed the producers that she had a role written specifically for her. An initial four-episode guest part proved so popular that she was quickly brought in as a regular character, and within the year Bernice Blackstock had become the first landlady of the Woolpack. Now Bernice is a core character, and her mother, sister and long-lost father have joined her in the series. Bernice has had a busy three years, involving, amongst other things, the difficulties of running the Woolpack with Tricia and a couple of Dingles on the staff, a stormy engagement to a bisexual oil-rig worker, a troubled marriage to the village vicar, a miscarriage and most recently a steamy affair with her sister's boyfriend. Just in the last few weeks, Samantha has been the subject of a prime-time ITV profile and appeared on the front cover of the *TV Times*. Put like that, it sounds almost like a fairytale career, but there is, of course, a bit more to it....

'I realized I wanted to be an actress when I was very, very little. In infant school, when I was five or six. I'd always enjoyed game playing, where I was doing a television programme or a radio programme. I was always trying to entertain, even as a child. Making up stories, pretending to be different people. So when I went to school properly (we did drama from when we were very young), I realized that it was what I liked doing. And I equated that with being an actor.

'I don't come from a showbiz family. My mother trained as a hairdresser, my father was a fireman. My mother's a great entertainer and storyteller, but I don't think she could ever get up in front of a camera and perform.

'I did a Drama and English degree at Bristol. I didn't have a career in acting in mind at the time, because as I got older, to say you want to be an actor at school seems such a bizarre thing. I lived in a rural part of Kent, and if I said I wanted to be an actress, everyone would ask me what I really wanted to do. It's one of those things, like wanting to be an astronaut – someone has to do it, so if you want it you should pursue that dream. But I thought I wasn't good enough.

When I first went to university, there were so many people there who were very confident, and wanted to be actors, and I lost a lot of confidence. It was only after I left that I ended up doing a play written by a friend from university, Matthew Westwood, who now writes for *Emmerdale,* and he'd written a part for me. We did that in the Edinburgh Festival, and I realized when I was rehearsing that I'd always wanted to be an actress, so why give up on it?

'It was terribly difficult. Not having gone to drama school I had no preparation, I knew nothing. I knew I had to get an agent. But you ring round all the agents, and they don't want to know, they are inundated with letters and people sending naff old photos and CVs with nothing on them, and they aren't interested. It's so cut-throat, and that's the first thing that made me realize how difficult it is. I ended up ringing someone and being really cheeky and they took me on. He was a terrible agent, got me no interviews whatsoever. But at least I had an agent, and so people took me a bit more seriously. Eventually we did the play, and it did fantastically. On the back of that I got offered a radio pilot – weirdly it was written by Peter Kerry, who's also now an *Emmerdale* writer. That didn't get picked up, we just did the pilot. After that, I thought things were going to take off, and they did for a moment, then nothing happened.

'But I just knew I was so absolutely determined, so convinced I would get there eventually. I had a two-year period where I worked as an actor for one day, but I just couldn't give up because there was nothing else I wanted to do.

'In 1995 I did a film with Rob Lowe [*Midnight Man,* a thriller based on a Jack Higgins novel] and I thought it would be my big break. It was shown on terrestrial TV all round the world, but unfortunately it was only shown on Sky over here. And that was very disappointing, because it was a fantastic part, very different to Bernice. I thought I'd hit the big time.

'Just before I got the *Emmerdale* audition, I was working at Habitat, which is where I met my husband. I went up for Tricia in June 1998. It's quite funny, I remember sitting in reception here at Emmerdale, and Sheree Murphy was there with her mum. I'd read about the character, and had a picture in my head and I remember looking at Sheree and thinking, "She's Tricia, she's just like I pictured her." I thought I was too old for the part, because Tricia's meant to be twenty, or something, and I was mid-twenties, and Sheree looked more innocent and naïve, just like the character was. So I thought I'm not right for it. The screen test was with Billy Hartman, who plays Terry Woods; I was trying on a dress. I was very nervous, I couldn't speak. Kieran Roberts, the producer at the time, tried to have a preliminary chat with me, but I was just opening my mouth and no sound was coming out. He must have thought I was a right idiot, but as soon as the camera was on me, I was fine, and the test went all right. (I'm sure I'd die of embarrassment if I saw it now, though.) Sheree got the part, so I was a bit disappointed, but not too surprised.

Then in August I was on holiday in Boston. I hadn't had a holiday in years. I was on the beach and I got a call saying that *Emmerdale* had another character, called Bernice, that they wanted me to play. They liked me, but didn't think I was right for Tricia. So I had four episodes, which was fantastic, and from that they offered me a longer-term contract.

'I jumped at it. It was just a dream to have regular work. To get my teeth into something, make it my own.

'Everyone was very welcoming. That's what's so nice about *Emmerdale*, there's such a good atmosphere. It's a terrible cliché, but the cast and crew are like a big family. If there is anyone that comes in and starts bigging it up, then they soon get cut down to size. They either get written out, or somebody tells them, because there's no room for that. This is a very pressurized schedule, we have to work, we all have to give our best, one hundred percent, and we want to do the job well. There's no room for prima donnas. Acting isn't about that – that's "celebrity". Acting is about teamwork, working together.

'It can be hard work. The women get in earlier than the men – we're in makeup for an hour, the men just go in for a light dusting. The working day is often twelve hours, and I've been extremely busy lately – it's been twelve-hour days for a long time. (Luckily, I've got two weeks' holiday coming.) It's good to have big stories, of course – I've been really, really fortunate. Part of that is working behind the bar – you're bound to be in more episodes because it's such a focal point. Plus I've had big storylines in the last three years.

'It can be difficult to plan character development, because you often need to know what happens next in the story in order to know how to play something. But if you think about it, in real life you don't know what's going to happen next, so the only thing you can do is play it truth-fully, in the moment. The only problem is when scripts seem to contradict what's gone before. So, take Bernice's affair with Carlos: a couple of blocks before, she was really in love with Carlos; then after Bernice decides to make a go of it, suddenly she can't bear to be with him. It's difficult, because it negates the whole story. So I did have a chat with Steve [Frost, the producer] about it. It's difficult to change things, but we tried to bring a bit more tenderness to it, say the same words, but show that they do care for and love each other. She can't deal with the reality of the situation – she loves him, but she's guilty about hurting Ashley. It's the right relationship at the wrong time.

'It has changed my life, yes. If I hadn't got the part, I'd be doing some other acting. I don't know what, but I'd still be acting.

'It takes a while to get into the public consciousness. It took a few months before people starting noticing me. People stare, more than anything. You certainly get recognized more up here than at home. The higher profile you are, the bigger your stories, the more you get recognized, until it becomes extremely difficult to go out sometimes. You can't go out in Leeds and be left alone.

'It's really weird, because people think they know you, because you're on the television and you're in their living rooms every night. They call you "Bernice", they expect you to act like her. It's very strange – I'm quite a private person, and if you don't get to know people that easily, then it's weird when someone talks to you like they're your friend. You feel such a phoney, because you're nice to them, and it's great they watch the programme and like it, but I can't be myself with them, because they don't know me. It can be intrusive sometimes, particularly if you're in the middle of a conversation with someone, or in the supermarket looking terrible. You can be in a bad mood, or just don't feel like it, and people just stare and whisper things. That can be quite difficult.

'I remember going to the first Soap Awards, and I'd only

been in the show about five months. My husband and I were just getting there in the car, and I didn't fancy going in straight away, so we thought we'd hang around outside for five minutes. When we arrived there were crash barriers and crowds of people, and they all started shouting "Bernice! Bernice!" and I was absolutely staggered. They knew me. I can't describe how unexpected it was. I'm so stupid, of course there would be people there, waiting to see famous people like Barbara Windsor and June Brown. Not me.

'I hate that word, "star". Everyone wants to be a star, but it's such an awful expression. I don't feel famous. Paul McCartney is famous, Mother Teresa was. I'm not, I'm well-known in the pockets of this country that watch *Emmerdale*.

'Financially it's good, but it's not the sort of money you see reported in the press. I have a huge problem when you see it reported in the papers that the Soapstars will be on £200,000 a year, and they quote people's wages, and we're not on that sort of money, not at all. It's good money, but nothing like that. Some of the people, a very few of them, on *Coronation Street* and *EastEnders* are. But the reports are ridiculous and out of proportion.

'I don't have a big house with a swimming pool, but I don't have to worry about paying my bills. If I'm shopping, I know I can buy things. I've never been into designer labels or spending thousands on clothes, but I can buy nice shampoo, not own-brand. My husband and I can get a mortgage – before that I'd always rented, and was just scraping by. I've got savings! But it's not flashy cars and living in Hollywood. My lifestyle's similar to anybody in an ordinary job who's earning a decent wage.

'The most enjoyable thing is working regularly doing what you want to do. There are so many people who leave school who don't know what they want to do with their lives, and I was fortunate in that I knew what I wanted to do and now I'm doing a job I love.

'The least enjoyable is the privacy thing. It's stuff like if you're having a row, you can't have it in public. Or if you want to go out for the evening and have an in-depth conversation with someone, you can't, because you're just not left alone. You have to go round to their house or they come round to yours, otherwise you get disturbed and people listen in. It comes with the territory, so I can't complain about it.

'I've been very lucky with the press, touch wood. When something does turn up in the papers, everyone here's very supportive of each other, there's no backbiting, or people being secretly pleased. This sort of thing happens in people's lives, for everyone. Because we're on television, ours gets talked about in public, whereas most people's doesn't, so we're no different to anyone else. Just because we're on the telly doesn't mean we live perfect lives or never do anything that's wrong. We all make mistakes. I don't think you can say "that person should have thought more about it if they're going to be on television", because we're all human.

'It worries me a bit. When there are cameras around, you watch yourself. If the cameras got into the green room, everyone would think we're all having affairs. It's very tactile, people hug each other – it's a very actorly thing, people just don't behave like that in other professions. So you're very aware. You give someone a hello kiss, it gets in the papers, and it ends up looking like everyone's having sex with each other. It's just them trying to dig up gossip.

'My family really love it. My mum thinks it's wonderful that I get recognized, she gets really excited. But she doesn't live with it day to day, and so to her it is quite exciting.

'I'm close to all my on-screen family, I'm incredibly lucky they are all so nice. I clicked with Liz [Estensen] as soon as she arrived, so hopefully it's convincing that we're mother and daughter. Patrick [Mower]'s lovely, he's such a kind, generous person and terribly thoughtful. My real parents don't feel threatened, or that their position is being usurped, they're fine with it. It's difficult for them, because they see it as me, it's their daughter, not Bernice.

'You do begin to think that the character starts to take you over. I don't act more like Bernice, she doesn't act more like me, but what you're playing, what's happening to her, it starts to affect me. Up in Leeds I live in a rented flat, it's not my home, so I'm alone and I can't always shake it off. This year, with sad things like the miscarriage and the affair starting, and the tears, it does start to eat you away, and you can feel very low sometimes. And there's always another script to learn, it's a bit like a sausage factory.

'I'm very good at learning lines, it doesn't take long. I've got a very good memory, touch wood. But also the more you use your brain to do that, it's like a muscle, the stronger it gets, you can keep it all in. When I come back from a holiday it can be difficult to get back into the swing of it.

'Technically I knew quite a lot before I came, but you never stop learning. It's certainly so much more natural for me now. People forget that the technical side is important – finding the light, hitting the mark, leaving beats where you need to, knowing where the camera is. All the time making it look like you're just talking in the pub. There are many different things to remember.

'You need to have holidays. Sometimes you get a bit low, if you're really tired. But I always have to remember that it's what I've always wanted to do, to be acting and working regularly, so the good far outweighs the bad.

'It's not a job for life. The whole nature of acting is to play different characters, so at some point I would want to do other stuff. But *Emmerdale*'s been fantastic for me, it's the nicest thing I've ever worked on, the people are great, and I'm lucky that I've got a really good character I'm playing.

profile 2: patrick mower

Patrick Mower has been a star of stage, film and television since the early Sixties, and was a heart-throb in the Seventies, when he was a regular in the series *Callan, Special Branch* and *Target*. He's had dozens of guest roles, in shows such as *The Avengers* (in which his character had a dastardly plan to impose a new single currency on Europe!), *Space 1999*, *The Sweeney* and *Minder*, and has starred in films as diverse as *The Devil Rides Out* and *Carry on England*. He's also appeared on panel games, including *Whodunnit!* and *Countdown*. Since last year, he's been a regular in *Emmerdale*, as Rodney Blackstock, the long-lost father of Woolpack landlady Bernice.

'I was very lucky. I started off as an amateur actor when I was eleven, I started an apprenticeship as a draughtsman when I was fifteen, and then at seventeen I auditioned for RADA and I got in, and everyone advised me to finish my apprenticeship, which I did. By the time I was twenty, I was in five different drama groups in Oxford, and so I was already a fairly decent actor, and I gained a scholarship at RADA. Before I left RADA, I got the lead in a musical, called *House of Cards*, at the Phoenix Theatre and went straight from that to working with Donald Wolfit in *John Gabriel Borkman* by Ibsen. Then I was in *Alfie*, so the West End was like my rep company. At the time it didn't occur to me, but looking back it was a pretty sensational start.

'I don't remember the first time anyone asked for my autograph. It sounds strange to say, but I seem to have been famous all my life. I've been in so many TV series, starting with *Front Page Story* and *Haunted*. They were "starring Patrick Mower". So I've been heading the bill for a long time. I think one of the reasons it's never affected me is that in my apprenticeship I was working in factories and press shops, and getting up at seven in the morning. A proper man's job. So I knew that being an actor was a good life.

'I'm not worried about being only known for being Rodney. I learnt a lesson from *Callan*, because people were always stopping Edward Woodward in the street and saying "Mister Callan, Mister Callan, could you sign this?" And that got to him. I've tried to make sure I was known as Patrick Mower, in every series I've done. I only did twenty-six episodes of *Special Branch*, I only did twenty-six of *Callan*, same with *Target*. I made sure the character never became more famous than Patrick Mower. Even now, even though twelve million viewers a night see me on *Emmerdale*, no one's ever stopped me in the street and called me "Rodney".

'That doesn't mean I see *Emmerdale* as a short-term commitment. I've just been asked to do another year, and I readily agreed. I don't look at it as short-term at all. It's perfectly possibly to keep my own character, my own persona, and still play Rodney Blackstock. And I don't see any problem with that at all. It's a great programme to work on. It's quite hard. You have to keep on top of it. It's like being an athlete, you've got to be ready when called. It's not glamorous, it's not easy. There's no star system, if you don't know your lines, it doesn't matter who you are.

'I don't know what happened, but I was offered parts in two other soaps at the same time I was offered *Emmerdale*, I'd better not say which ones. So there was something in the air. It might have been that they'd heard on the grapevine that I was interested in doing a soap.

'I became an actor because I love acting. That's why I do it. Every day on *Emmerdale* I've got different lines, I have new storylines. If I was in a West End play, it would be the same script every night, and sometimes you go, "Oh God, I've got to go and do that again." I've never thought, "Oh God, I've got to go and do Rodney." Even if you're doing a drama, you do thirteen episodes, or you do a film, then you're only actually there for a few weeks, that's all you do. The rest of the time you're not working. That's an actor's life. But you're not acting. I like acting. This way, I'm doing what I want to do, all the time.

'I'm fascinated by the way a new character gets grounded in an existing show, how they write it so I'm bedded in. I'm very happy with the way things have gone on *Emmerdale*.'

the home straight

CHAPTER EIGHT

Thursdy 30 August to Friday 31 August, 2001.
The finals are in the closing stages. Tears as the
judges get it down to two hopefuls for each role.

day three

Day three of the final starts off at another location that the
new family will frequently be seen in, the Emmerdale
Holiday Village. The holiday village is actually a long-estab-
lished part of the programme, first seen back in 1991,
when it was opened by Frank Tate. It's provided a good
rationale to bring newcomers for short stays in the village,
and it's a handy way to get a lot of the teenage characters
working together in the same stories and scenes. It also
allows *Emmerdale* to show off some of the Yorkshire countryside, and to involve leisure pursuits, such as pony
trekking. It was phased out by the last producer of
Emmerdale, Kieran Roberts, who was keen to make the most
of the new village. It hasn't been seen in the series since the
summer of 1998 (when one of the teenage staff was played
by Danielle Brown, the younger sister of Spice Girl Mel B),
although it's been mentioned from time to time.

In terms of the fiction, the holiday village is close to the
Home Farm estate, and has been run by the Tate family up
to now, but Patrick Mower's character, Rodney Blackstock,
has taken a stake in the place, with Chris Tate, and hopes

to make money from the venture. Rodney brings in the parents of the new family to run the Holiday Village... not quite realizing that they've only recently become a couple, or that they've got three disgruntled children in tow.

At the studio, back in Leeds, the interior of one of the chalets has been lovingly recreated as the new family home. It's far easier to shoot scenes in the controlled environment of the studio, and it saves a great deal of time (and money) if they do so. Besides, the chalets are quite small – it's a squeeze fitting all five family members in, let alone any other characters who are in the scene and a whole Outside Broadcast crew.

But the outside scenes will be filmed at Rudding Park, a real holiday park, not far from the Emmerdale village set. *Emmerdale* have leased two of the chalets to be used in the series, and these sit in a wood, by the side of a small ornamental lake, which is full of ducks and waterlilies. This is the first public outing for the finalists. The holiday season hasn't quite finished yet. Most of the other chalets still have young families in them. At the sight of a film crew, a small crowd gathers in the distance. *Soapstars* hasn't started airing yet, so no one recognizes the panel or any of the finalists. That doesn't stop a group of children from asking some of the finalists for their autographs, though.

It's fair to say that Paul de Freitas isn't in his element.

Both he and Yvon are worried about their shoes in the mud. Paul's unconvinced that people really do come here for their holidays. However, most of the finalists appreciate the tranquillity of the place after the hectic lives they've been leading since June.

Nicola Orr stands by the bank of the small lake, and looks out. She really wants to work here now. Most of the other finalists didn't watch *Emmerdale* until a few weeks ago, but Nicola's been a fan for as long as she can remember, and gives people a potted history of the holiday village. When she was three, her parents tell her, she'd think that the people on TV actually lived in the TV. 'I still want to live in the TV,' she admits. She'd love to work with Samantha Giles. If she got the part, she'd want it for life – she sees herself going from teenaged daughter to replacing Betty, the nosy pensioner who props up the Woolpack bar. Nicola is the only finalist left who's not been paid for some acting work. No one in her family works in the entertainment industry, but she's studied acting and dance. As they all wait to be called, she relaxes by running through a dance routine with Ruth – and Jason joins in from the sidelines. Erin guesses, correctly, that Jason's had some dance training. Erin has been a professional dancer for over 20 years, and wants to move away from musicals to television acting. She's surprised to get this far, and confesses she thinks she's out of her league.

It's all very real for the finalists now. For the first time, the *Soapstars* crew outnumber the hopefuls. They're down to the last three for each role, they all know they're in with a chance of coming back here in a few weeks and doing the scenes for real. Johnny Kinch can't wait – he wants to get in a fight with Cain Dingle, he wants to push someone in the lake. Dee Whitehead's feeling relaxed – she can see herself working here now. For a lot of the finalists, this week has spelt out just how hard the job's going to be, but it's also convinced them that they could be good enough.

There's a light schedule today – half the group will do a scene here, the other half will do a scene later that morning with Patrick Mower. Some of the younger actors aren't sure who Patrick Mower is, but Dee and Debra are, and are looking forward to it.

For half the people here, there's nothing to do but wait, and try to relax. By the end of the day, another five of them will be out. At this stage in proceedings, whoever goes will be good. Erin is, as has now become traditional, convinced this is her last day. Some of the finalists try to guess who's going to win – it should be an easy choice, now, but no one's entirely confident of success, or of predicting success for others. Dee and Johnny are popular bets; beyond that, people are non-committal. This week has proved to be a confidence booster for nearly all of them. It's proved that, even if they don't win, they've got a chance of making a go of television acting. It's good experience; they've made good contacts.

Huddled in one of the chalets, the judges are firming up their opinions. The scenes they are watching today are the actual lines, in the actual locations, that the winners will be performing, and it's made it clear to them that some of the actors, even very good ones, aren't right for the part. The judges are getting a very firm idea of their favourites – while nothing's in the bag yet, they've pretty much decided today that Jason and Ruth should get the parts they are up for – but there are still areas of doubt.

They think the mum should be Erin or Dee, but they really can't decide between the two. With the dads, it's even more dramatic. Yvon's really starting to see the qualities of Mark Jardine. 'I'm having to back-pedal furiously,' she tells the other judges. Mark himself picked up on the vibes: 'I'll tell you the turning point – it was the third day of the finals. All along, I'd known Yvon was really keen on Johnny Kinch, and she was thinking about whether she fancied us or not.

Not in an unprofessional way – she just knew that people want to watch that. And I don't think I was ever Mr Sexy to her. But at the Holiday Village she came up to me and asked if I'd cut my hair. I hadn't, but I told her I had, and then from the very next scene I did, I heard her say, "He's good" about me, and I think she was starting to see me as a bit sexy.'

It's still a three-way contest, though – Bill's worried about Brian: 'He just doesn't seem motivated this week.' Yvon agrees: 'His confidence is completely shot.' Bill's sympathetic, but points out that he's been like that for three days now – 'If this was the show, he'd have cocked up three whole episodes in that time.'

The judges are agreed that Ruth is one of the two daughters, but the other one is a tough choice. They have decided that Gemma will have to lose out to a strong field, but beyond that.... Paul thinks Jo-Ann's good, and he loves Nicola, but he doesn't think they can use her for the part. It's not over yet, but the judges are getting closer to a final conclusion.

The group is barely at the holiday park for ninety minutes before the scenes are done. They return to the coach, and Trinity College, for the second half of the scenes.

By now, of course, the judges have got a good handle on the abilities of the remaining finalists, and they've got pretty firm opinions. It's still useful to see them in new scenes – it's allowing them to try out various combinations of family members, to see how the actors work together. These are scenes featuring the actual characters they'll be playing, either in the location they'll be playing them in, or with the existing cast member they'll be playing them with. It's as close as you can get to the real thing.

Before the second batch of scenes, the finalists meet Patrick Mower and have a fairly informal question-and-answer session. They're preoccupied by the looming decision – Patrick warns them that rejection is part of an actor's life. However, he assures them that if they're good enough, they'll be welcomed with open arms by the existing cast.

By now, though, the finalists are asking about practicalities – how long before filming do they get the scripts? (about two weeks); how much rehearsal time do they get? (none, really – a read-through on set, then a camera rehearsal, then a take); how many takes for each scene? (one, hopefully, two usually, rarely more than three); what about bad publicity? (no one takes it that seriously, it's not what they are there for). Patrick's keen to stress that he's having one of the happiest times of his life on the programme, and that it's a very creative process.

Patrick and the finalists begin running through the scene – again, it's from the first episode featuring the family. Rodney is showing the family the chalet they'll be living in. And the children aren't impressed....

RODNEY: *This is where you'll be living.*

JESS: *It's like a shed.*

LUCY: *There's only two bedrooms.*

MAGGIE: *You and Jess can share.*

LUCY: *I'm not sharing.*

JESS: *That makes two of us.*

[Jess goes back outside and Lucy slams the bedroom door shut]

PHIL: *I don't suppose you've got anywhere bigger?*

RODNEY: *I'm afraid not. All the chalets are the same size.*

PHIL: *It's going to be a squash.*

RODNEY: *I had no idea there would be so many of you.*

PHIL: *I suppose we ought to explain.*

MAGGIE: *Yes.*

RODNEY: *Explain what?*

MAGGIE: *It's complicated. We've been in other relationships.*

PHIL: *This is our first day as a couple. A family.*

MAGGIE: *We've wanted to be together for a long time. Getting this job gave us the incentive to make the break. It's all happened very suddenly.*

RODNEY: *I hope it works out for you. But I'm only interested in how well you do the job.*

MAGGIE: *Don't worry. It's a big chance for us. We won't let you down.*

Patrick tries to keep it as close as possible to the way they'd do the scene in *Emmerdale* – an informal run-through of lines, to check everyone's OK with the scene, then a proper run-through, followed by a take.

Everyone's a little nervous – this is their last chance to impress, after all – and a little tired, but by now they're used to doing this sort of scene. They complete the scenes, and break for lunch.

Outside, Tim Miller tries to film Patrick's view of what he's just seen. There are a couple of sound problems – they aren't far from Leeds/Bradford airport, and planes keep going overhead. One of the builders is doing some hammering – he's already asked for £30 to stop. Another builder has taken rather a shine to Erin. What's more, it's also threatening to rain.

Eventually, they can film the interview. Patrick's concerned – he's aware he's in an awkward position here. He doesn't want to criticize anyone, in case he's working with them next month, and he doesn't want to praise anyone who's on the way out, for the same reason. By now, Tim's got a good idea of who's likely to make it through to the last ten, but he's keeping very quiet – he wants to keep as much of a lid on the result as possible. Patrick and Tim edge around each other... who did Patrick like? Patrick was keen on Jo-Ann. Tim tells him it will be fine to mention Jo-Ann. Patrick also thought Jason had something. Tim smiles, then quickly says that would be fine, too.

Patrick does the interview, praising Jo-Ann and Jason's performances. Tim gets his interview in the can. And just as they're finished, it starts raining.

The finalists are tense now.

They've completed the audition process. It's hard to believe that they've done all they have to do. Brian and Erin are worried that they've fallen at the last hurdle – they didn't think they did well today. Jo-Ann's looking at the other finalists, and is convinced she doesn't fit. She's half-Indian, half-Portuguese, and everyone else who's left is white. Despite assurances all along that this won't be an issue (and despite the fact Erin's also part-Indian), she's not convinced. Dee's philosophical – even if she doesn't make it, she's had a big boost in confidence.

After an hour's lunch, the finalists are brought into the Blue Room and discover how they are to be told their fate – they'll go in to see the judges one by one, but after

TIM MILLER, *Soapstars* producer

'No, it wasn't difficult to talk to people when you know they're in or out. You get used to it very quickly. It's part of the job and something we have to do on lots of programmes we work on. We've got the poker-face down to an art. It's a vital part of the programme-maker's armoury.'

that there will have to be a degree of separation – they don't want anyone to be able to work out how they've done by comparing notes. It'll be easy enough to do, because only one person up for each role is being dropped at this stage.

Rejection now is going to be tough to take. The finalists all know each other very well by this point, and they've also got friends among the crew and even the judges. Tim Miller admits: 'Yes, we had our favourites. In fact, before the finals we had an office sweep-stake. I won, getting three out of the five. Sharon also got three out of five. But I have been forced to hand back the cash on the grounds that I had the ear of Steve Frost and was being fed tips.'

Up until now, the hopefuls have all accepted the stage where some of them are eliminated with good grace. It's been tense; people have, naturally enough, become upset they are going, or to see friends go, but they have been happy to go through with the process.

Today is different.

The mood has quickly become darker, more fraught. Jason's singing to himself in the corner. Erin, Jo-Ann and Ruth are all getting upset at the waiting. Johnny and Craig are pacing around, restless. Elspeth is frustrated with the wait. Most of the others, however they've coped, are very subdued.

The judges are taking their time to talk to people, and then the camera crews are filming the finalists' reactions and giving them a short interview. It means the process is taking longer than expected. Because not everyone is returning to the hall, it's impossible to know exactly who's in and out, and how people are coping with the news. The previous rounds have seen whoops of delight, group hugs, lots of backslapping and displays of commiseration or congratulation. This time, for some reason, it's almost sombre. Perhaps that's because the stakes are higher, or because it's all too close to call, or because the people are tired, or simply because there are so very few people left that it's difficult to muster a group spirit when a few of them are out of the room. For whatever reason, the atmosphere is heavy.

Since Patrick Tucker's advice, everyone's more conscious of the cameras. The hopefuls have known the score since the beginning – there have been cameras pointing at them from the start, registering every reaction.

Now it starts to get to them. One of the girls is crying, and a DV crew hurry over to record it. Johnny sees what they're about to do and grabs the lens – how dare they intrude? How do they *think* she feels? Can't they see that the last thing she wants is a camera in her face?

Was Tim Miller worried about being intrusive? 'No, it didn't worry me at all. Everyone accepted that we would film the highs and the lows. Even when people were very upset they still did interviews with us.' Indeed, Tim can see some positive advantages to the situation: 'I think that when people are distraught it can sometimes help for them to talk to someone impartial. It's often easier than talking to someone who offers lots of sympathy. It's no more intrusive to film someone's tears of disappointment than it is to

> **TIM MILLER, *Soapstars* producer**
>
> 'It is impossible in a short programme featuring dozens of people to portray a totally rounded view of an individual's character – so yes, we will focus in on one thing, but not in a way that would be unfair to them.'

film their tears of joy. Everyone knew the score because they'd all seen *Popstars*. We never tried to disguise what we were doing. We were up-front, which is why the hopefuls were up-front.

'The ITC code (the rules laid down by the television regulator) puts us under an obligation to treat people fairly. An adjudication against you by the ITC is a very serious matter, as the regulator has the power to fine TV companies hundreds of thousands of pounds, and even take their licence away. So we do take the code very seriously.

'What we do try and do is ensure that viewers can identify with characters and will remember them. So, for instance, if someone sneaks past the London queue (Dean Abrahams) or hands in a box with their CV in it at the auditions (Craig Henderson), then we will repeatedly remind people of this. Or, for instance, we always saw Sarah Smart in the context of someone who had forgotten her lines.'

If it was fraught in the audition hall, it's often no better with the judges. Yvon's on the verge of tears. Bill's clearly very downcast. Paul tells Nicola she's not made it through, and she's extremely upset. The judges hear her crying outside, which upsets them in turn. Paul's emotional when he tells Dean, whom he's described as 'his discovery', that he's not going any further. He explains, 'Normally when you're casting you don't get attached to people. We've all had laughs with the people here, got to know about their families… so we've all got a bit choked up to say "no" to some of them.' Bill has every sympathy: 'They've been through a lot – it's months since the first audition, now, and to not know where you're at for that long – it's about as much pressure as they're ever going to face.'

News starts filtering back – Elspeth's angry that she can work out she's through, because by now she knows that two of the daughters, Gemma and Nicola, are out.

Debra Michaels is out.

One of the last to learn his fate is Johnny Kinch – who's out. It's the result that surprises the most people in the hall. Johnny's disappointed, but still confident that this will lead to other things. Yvon was continuing to champion Johnny – 'He's been my fab fave all along' – but Bill's been sceptical for just as long: 'He's an *EastEnders* actor, he wouldn't work.' Paul's gradually been persuaded by Bill that Johnny doesn't fit the brief, and Steve and Keith's agreement with Bill has sealed his fate. Having seen Johnny playing actual scenes in the character of the new dad, with the potential daughters, Yvon was convinced to change her mind.

Everyone reassembles in the hall. People are still a little dazed, shocked to be through, upset to be out, trying to piece together who their rival is, and who else could make up their family.

The ten people through to this stage are going to come in tomorrow for one last session in front of the judges. But tomorrow, no one's going to be eliminated. This will be a last chance to impress, before the final decision.

day four

It's down to ten finalists, two for each role:

☐ Phil, the dad of the family, will be Mark Jardine or Brian McDevitt.

☐ His daughter, Jess, the eldest, will be Ruth Abram or Elspeth Brodie.

☐ Maggie, the mum of the family, will be played by either Erin Lordan or Dee Whitehead.

☐ Her son, Craig, will be either Jason Hain or Craig Henderson.

☐ Her daughter, Lucy, the youngest, will be either Jo-Ann D'Costa or Becky Weeks.

Once again, Jo-Ann has applied for a TV job, made it through a field of thousands and got down to the last two. It's vindicated her decision to pass on the CITV audition to be here... but she's not got the job yet. 'I want to come first,' she says eagerly. 'I'm so fed up of coming second.' She still doesn't think there's a potential family for her to fit in with, though.

Erin's relaxed a little, now that she's through to the last two. She's spent almost twenty years performing, but as a dancer, a singer, in musicals. Getting this far in the *Soapstars* process has helped to convince her that she could be a television actress. She's not sure she's got the role – it depends what the judges are looking for. Characteristically, she's assuming the worst, and is emphasizing the fluffed lines earlier. She doesn't relish the three-week wait until the result's announced.

With only ten finalists here, setting out chairs now barely takes any time at all, and everyone, from actors to crew, spends a fair amount of the day wondering where everyone else is.

There's very little on the agenda today, as far as the finalists are concerned. They run through another scene, this time with Jude Dyne, an *Emmerdale* director. The judges watch, but by now they've got a shrewd idea who they want. This session is to help confirm that instinct, to steady any last-minute doubts. They ask for a couple of specific things – they want to see Dee get angry, for example, because she usually seems so calm. She gets Mark Jardine to put more pace into his performance. All the time the judges watch not just the performance, but how well the actors take direction. Everyone's tired. For the first time, Erin, Dee and Ruth fluff lines, which panics them a little – have they fallen at the last hurdle?

Tim Miller fills the finalists in with the schedule for the next few weeks – the judges will come to their final decision at some point in the next fortnight. Three weeks from now, camera crews and one of the judges will visit every one of the homes of the last ten hopefuls, and they'll break the news there. Before then, the current plan is that a crew will pop by in a week or so to film them all at home, to get more of an idea of their backgrounds. Tim warns people to keep very quiet about getting this far – in the internet era, it would be quite possible for everyone to know who got to the last ten before the first programme has even been broadcast.

With the finalists sent away, the judges congregate and make a provisional decision.

They all agree it was good to see the family scenes, and it's helped crystallize a few opinions. The first order of business is picking a mum.

Paul thinks that Dee is 'the safe, cosy, warm, motherly one', while Erin's got 'sex appeal, lots of potential'. They agree Erin and Mark were a good combination. Bill's made up his mind: 'We don't need potential at this stage, we need actual – Dee's competent and consistent.' Yvon's torn – 'Erin's sexy and out there... but Dee's glam, too. Comfy glam. Which way do we want to go? Will Erin look old enough to be the mother of teenaged kids?' Bill reminds them that she worked well with Patrick Mower, but so did Dee. He knows who he wants.

Paul reckons that Mark has now proved himself much stronger than Brian. Yvon's not so sure – 'It's a tough choice. They are strong for different reasons. Mark's consistently strong, a tad on the boring side. He's the safe option.' Bill thinks Brian's been weak in the finals, but reminds them how impressed they all were at the semis – 'He's suffering from nerves, that's all.'

Choosing the daughters is the toughest decision of the lot – 'They're good girls, whoever goes, it's such a tough field,' as Bill says. 'I'm dreading telling them,' admits Yvon. They quickly agree that Ruth's going to be one of them – 'I'm ecstatic,' says Paul, 'She's been strong all along, she's probably the strongest actress we've seen.' Paul's now wavering towards Becky as the other daughter 'She's been so much better at this stage.' Bill thinks Jo-Ann's 'got a lovely smile, and she's good on camera'. They're also loathe to lose Elspeth – 'She's a good actress, but does she fit the brief?' It's a shame she'll lose out to Ruth. Bill reminds them she's young enough to play Lucy – and once that's done, the comparison becomes easier: they think Becky and Jo-Ann are 'no real competition'.

With the boys, they're torn between 'safe' Craig and 'risky' Jason. Bill's not so sure: 'I don't see Jason as a risk.' Yvon agrees they're both good, it's just a question of who fits the brief best. Is Craig too old?

Three days before the first *Soapstars* show is broadcast, the die is cast.

the results

CHAPTER NINE

*'Dogstars' decides who will be the family dog, and
the transmission of* Soapstars *gets underway.*

The first episode of *Soapstars*, an hour-long special, was
broadcast on Monday 3 September, at 9.30 in the evening.

The three judges' first TV appearance together was
about twelve hours earlier, as guests of Twiggy on the first
post-Richard-and-Judy edition of *This Morning*. At this
stage, all the questions are about the initial fifteen seconds,
as are the articles in the TV listings pages.

The programme itself follows on from an hour and a
half of *Coronation Street*. Early the next morning, the
overnight ratings figures are in: *Soapstars* got a respectable
audience figure of 6.3 million, a 31.8 percent share of the
audience. Importantly, it also beat the opposition, getting
2 million more than *999* on BBC1, and 5 million more
than the first episode of the new series of *Coupling* on
BBC2. It's early days, but *Soapstars* has made a solid start.

A number of the finalists phone each other up. For a
few, seeing the clips and the judges on TV is the point at
which it finally sinks in: *Soapstars* is really happening. The
first show doesn't really feature any of the finalists –
there's a tiny glimpse of Johnny Kinch. But for the first
time, they get to hear some of the judges' deliberations,
and find out what they were looking for. The finalists look

for clues, to see if they can get any nearer predicting whether they've won. Elspeth Brodie notes, 'I was interested to hear afterwards what the judges said they didn't like, because I came on and acted all angry at them for having to wait in the queue, and I did a lot of pointing. So I was lucky, I guess.'

The *Soapstars* website goes up, with a 250-word summary of the first episode, as well as competitions and potted biographies of the judges. There is also an official internet message board, which buzzes into life the morning after the first broadcast. The main topic of conversation is Yvon's cutting remarks about the Bristol accent:

'I feel a bit flat about Bristol,' she had said. 'To be honest with you, I've got a problem with the accent in Bristol and, as a commercial drama person, I know that we're going to be looking for good-looking men and women. There's something about a Bristol accent; I don't think I'd ever be able to ask a nation to fancy someone from Bristol. I can't imagine having sex with someone from Bristol. I just think it's not a sexy accent.'

Unsurprisingly, the people of Bristol aren't impressed by this line of reasoning. This response on the message board is typical:

– I can't believe what that red-headed cow said about Bristol's accent.

– There's nothing wrong with it.

– She said about, she wouldn't want sex with anyone from Bristol.

– Well, I can't say anyone from Bristol would want sex with her, I mean we do have standards here you know, so she's got no chance! When she next comes to Bristol she'd better bring a lot of security because it was all over Bristol's papers tonight that there is going to be a lot of people there waiting for her – well if i can call her a "her"!

– YVONE – Nasty Nigel was as sweet as a puppy compared to you, you're just a stuck-up cow who can't get any sex, so don't go dissing Bristol, WE'RE GONNA GET YOU....

The message board soon proves popular – most of the contributors seem to be youngsters who attended the open auditions, looking to contact people they met on the day.

There are now to be ten programmes, going out on Mondays and Thursdays. The first three deal with the open auditions, the fourth covers the first day of the semi-finals (going down from seventy-two hopefuls to thirty-six), the fifth takes in the second two days of the semis (getting down from thirty-six to twenty-five), the sixth deals with the first two days of the finals (twenty-five become fifteen), with the seventh dealing with the rest of the final, and ending with the alternatives for each role (fifteen become ten). An eighth programme deals with the last day of the final, and profiles the ten remaining finalists. The ninth programme is an hour-long final, broadcast on Saturday 29 September, reminding people of the process, then going to each house in turn to see the decisions delivered. The tenth programme is *Nearly Soapstars* – a profile of people who fell before the last ten, including, by way of repentance, the people of Bristol.

And finally, a special episode goes out before the first episode of *Emmerdale* the new family appear in, on the night of 7 November.

On 20 September, episode six airs. Ashra Price takes part in a webchat on the official site about her experiences. The country has just seen her rejected at the end of Day Two of the final. She tells people it was a shame to get rejected after putting in so much effort, and investing so much time, and that the worst thing about the audition was being away from her son, Fox.

'dogstars'? you can't be sirius...

Tuesday 21 August and Friday 24 August
The new family are to have a pet dog, and – keeping with the *Soapstars* spirit – that dog will be chosen from an open audition, to be broadcast in a special programme, *Dogstars*, a couple of weeks after *Soapstars* itself finishes. Unlike the humans, the general public will get a say in the decision – the *Dogstars* programme will see judges narrow the field down to two dogs, and then there will be a phone-in vote, where the public will decide between them.

Bill, Paul and Yvon are confining their judging activities to the humans, and *Dogstars* has its own panel of experts:

DR ROGER MUGFORD is an internationally renowned animal psychologist who has written several popular books including *Dog Training The Mugford Way* and *Dr Mugford's Casebook*, spelling out how to apply behavioural therapy techniques to train problem animals. He's the founder of the Animal Behaviour Centre which has become the leading centre for the treatment of eccentric or problem behaviour in pets, and Animals in Court, a company that provides an expert witness service for any owner whose animal has landed them in legal trouble. He's used his techniques to tame some of the Queen's corgis. He's a frequent contributor to TV shows, such as *Countryfile*. Most recently, he's been involved with *Pig Brother*, an internet reality show in aid of farmers hit by foot-and-mouth, where pigs are voted out from a special sty.

GILL RADDINGS is an animal trainer who runs her own agency, Gill Raddings' Stunt Dogs. She started out by supplying the dogs who played the wolves in *A Company of Wolves*, and now her animals – mostly dogs – appear in many drama productions. She's the trainer of Wellard on *EastEnders* and Wee Jock in *Hamish Macbeth*. Recently she trained Russell Crowe's dog in *Gladiator*, which was allocated its own make-up artist, and the red setter that plays the piano in the Smirnoff adverts. All her dogs come from rescue shelters, and most live in family homes when they aren't filming.

PETER YOUNG runs Peter's Posh Pets, described as "the Vidal Sassoon of dogdom", and is an expert on dog grooming. He judges major dog shows here and in Ireland, has written a number of advice columns on the subject of dog grooming and care, and is the presenter of the video *Grooming for All Pet Dogs*.

The first day's events take place at the South Leeds Stadium. Unlike the process for casting the humans, *Emmerdale* want to make sure that the dog is from the area. They've placed adverts in the local papers and told local dog clubs. *Emmerdale* won't be taking anyone's dog away from them – it will continue to live with its owners, in the family home, but when required for the show it will be brought over to the village or studio sets. The owner will get paid for the use of their dog, and will also get a contribution towards its upkeep.

It's a wet Tuesday morning, and that seems to have kept away the crowds – in the event, only around fifty dogs have shown up. The first day's agenda is to run the dogs through a police agility run, to test their general fitness and level of training. The judges have been joined by Sue Beale, the animal trainer for *Emmerdale*. There are currently seven regular dogs on the show, and – as there's a vet's surgery in the village – there are often one-off appearances by cats. There are very few soap cats, for reasons that are obvious if you've ever owned one – they aren't easy to train, although both Sue and Jill have done so in the past.

Sue explains that the new dog isn't going to be required for any particularly gruelling or specialist purpose – it's a family dog, and will be seen on walks with the family, or sleeping on the sofa. It doesn't need special training in stuntwork, or to learn any particularly elaborate tricks, but it will have to be a dog that's well-behaved, and that can follow a few basic commands. As the humans found out over in *Soapstars*, if anyone fluffs a line or misses their mark, filming has to stop. The same applies for the family dog. As the dogs go through their routine, the judges quickly narrow the field down to six:

☐ Sally is owned by Jackie, and was a rescue dog.

☐ Murfi is a terrier, owned by Elaine.

☐ Bess is owned by John, and is one of two Border collies to make the final.

☐ Sercha is being looked after by Liz.

☐ Jack is the other Border collie, and his owner is also called John.

☐ Harry is a Labradoodle – half-labrador, half-poodle. It's an unlikely mix – he's the size of a labrador, but has the basic body shape of a poodle.

The dogs are sent off to learn three tasks to perform on command – to beg, bark and then crawl. Sue's not convinced that it's the ideal test for an *Emmerdale* dog. On a soap, a dog's job rarely extends beyond following its owner around on a walk, or sleeping on a sofa. But this test will demonstrate how quickly a dog can pick up training, and how obedient it is. The owners have two days to teach their dogs new tricks – and the *Soapstars* crew go round to check their progress on Thursday.

Friday morning sees a small crew prepare the Robert Craven Memorial Hall in Bramhope, near Leeds, for the *Dogstars* final. At ten o'clock Marnie Sirota, the production assistant, is sitting on the stage, sticking lots of little gold stars onto a big star-shaped piece of paper. There were meant to be six giant gold stars, one for each dog, but half of them have got lost in transit. There's a sheet of small star stickers, and she's making a big star from those; it's taking longer than she thought. This will, eventually, be the star that goes on Murfi's podium. The remaining two dogs will have to make do with smaller stars.

Meanwhile, Tom has gone off to find six roast chickens from somewhere, and the lighting crew are wondering how secure the glitterball is. 'They're surprisingly heavy,' one of them says, reassuringly, 'you'd know if it fell on you.' They're more impressed by the light in the hall – today is cloudy but bright, ideal conditions because the lighting level is even, and there's an enormous window at the other end of the hall that means the lighting crew's job is almost done for them.

There's not a vast amount of preparation to be done, but any TV show takes a while to set up. It will mean quite a lot of waiting around for the finalists and their owners, but this in itself is a good test – the winning dog will have a fair amount of waiting around on set to do. So, ironically, this could be the best test of the lot.

The dogs come down from the stage in turn, and perform their routine. Sally, the first up, behaves perfectly. Murfi chooses to sneeze rather than bark, but is otherwise spot on. Things start to go a little wrong from there – Bess is fine, but her owner gets a little confused. Harry does quite well, Sercha and Jack miss a couple of tricks.

After lunch, there's a test that's meant to replicate conditions on a busy set – a clapperboard, thunder, bright lights, a swinging boom, a doorbell, the sound of shots and… a roast chicken at the end.

It's not like any real set, of course, but it's perhaps a good test of temperament. Most of the dogs are unfazed by the distractions – although it's pretty obvious that some have learned to bark when the doorbell rings at home. Bess barely reacts at all (the judges praise her as 'resilient'); Sercha doesn't either. Murfi's well-behaved, but does lick at the chicken. Harry panics a little. Sally runs off with the chicken.

The judges convene upstairs – they make allowances for Sercha – their owner is away on holiday, and Liz doesn't have the same degree of control. But even so, Sercha failed to do any of their three tasks, and didn't make much of an impression during the second test. They're not convinced Sercha has 'star quality', and are a little disappointed in the collies, which are meant to be very trainable. Roger's surprised how 'sound reactive' Harry was, but is impressed by Murfi, a terrier – not thought to be one of the more trainable breeds. The judges are concerned by a practical problem with both Murfi and Harry – the camera won't do either of them justice. In person, Harry's very appealing, and has extraordinary eyebrows, but on camera he just looks like a silhouette. Murfi's very cute and obedient, but he's small, and it will be tricky for a director to frame a shot with him in, without an actor having to lean in or kneel down. The key to this process is that the winning dog won't cause any production problems like this. Both have performed well, and have the right temperament, but the judges agree that it doesn't translate to being a practical dog for a soap opera. Reluctantly, they eliminate them from the running.

So, it's down to the two Border collies and Sally. The judges have a few concerns with Bess, but on the whole feel she's got the edge over Jack.

The decision is made – the two dogs to face the public vote will be Bess and Sally. The owners are reconvened and told the news. The rest will be up to the public. Roger, a qualified human psychologist, reckons it's in the bag for Bess.

The programme is broadcast on 30 September, and the phone-in vote starts as soon as the show is over.

Bess wins.

and the winners are...

CHAPTER TEN

Friday 21 September to Sunday 23 September.
Soapstars *is broadcast, the winners are*
announced and set to work.

For a couple of weeks, only the judges, Steve Frost, Keith
Richardson, Tim Miller and the cameraman who filmed
the final judges' deliberation have known who the winners
are. No one on the *Soapstars* crew is told. Not even key
people at *Emmerdale* know – Karen Grimes, one of the two
script editors, has been avidly watching *Soapstars*, and
knows who she wants to win (and who she definitely does-
n't), but even she hasn't been told the result. 'Steve knows,
obviously, but he's not telling us. He's very pleased with
who's been cast, and he's given us a couple of hints – Jess
and Lucy are a little older than we were expecting, Craig's
a little younger. It has an effect on things – at story conference, someone will say one of them should have a crush on
a particular character, and Bill and Steve will say they're a
bit too old or young or whatever. I've been watching the
show, so I think I can work out who's won, but Steve's not
saying anything!'

If Karen's been watching, does she have her favourites?
'I hate to say it, but more often it's a case of hoping some

of the people won't get it. The finals are on TV this week, and I've been relieved to see a couple of people go.'

Lance Milligan, the *Emmerdale* costume designer, needed to know the actors' measurements, so he could get costumes ready for them. All ten finalists supplied their measurements, and Lance was given those of the winners, and a few days later some headshots, but not the names of the actors.

It is, of course, a tense time for the ten remaining finalists. Most keep in touch with each other. There are people who are quietly confident, people who are convinced they haven't got it, but no one knows for sure.

Erin thinks they'd made up their minds about some of the parts early on in the finals week. Becky thinks that's right – 'They definitely had by the time we were at the holiday village – they loved Ruth, and we got a bit sidelined.' Brian nods – 'I had such a bad week. I thought the panel had made up their mind, at least to get it down to Johnny and Mark, and I just wanted to go home, and I wasn't the only one... on the last day, right at the end, Paul wished me luck for the future, which I thought was a bit of a giveaway.' Jo-Ann says she quickly got the idea she wouldn't get the part – 'I just didn't look like anyone else.' Dee wasn't sure: 'They could have gone either way, Erin and I have different looks, and you just don't know.'

Erin's certain: 'I knew Dee had it, I said that right from the start. Paul always seemed to be smiling at Ruth, so I thought she was in.' Brian recognizes this: 'Paul was very friendly with Ruth, I barely talked to him.' Becky thought Ruth had it. Elspeth also thought she'd lost out to Ruth. Ruth denies she ever thought like that: 'There wasn't an inch of me that thought I'd got it.' Becky also overheard the judges saying they liked the Scottish accent, so guessed they'd also go for Elspeth. Craig also didn't think he'd get it: 'I thought it would get down to Dean and Jason – I know I can't play twenty-one.' Is anyone going to say they thought it was in the bag? Jason admits, 'I thought I was nearer the brief than Craig.' Mark's more forthcoming – 'If I had to choose between Brian and me, I'd pick me.'

The weekend before the winners are announced in the 29 September hour-long special, three crews set out to the finalists' houses, each with one of the judges, to deliver the news. Whatever the result, they can't tell anyone except close family. There's to be intense secrecy, right up until next Friday night – after that, it's too late for the papers to print the result before it's announced on television. In the event, the official website accidentally reveals the result on Saturday morning, before the offending page is quickly removed.

So, the new family are:

❏ Phil, the dad of the family – Mark Jardine

❏ Maggie, the mum – Dee Whitehead

❏ Jess, the elder daughter – Ruth Abram

❏ Craig, the son – Jason Hain

❏ Lucy, the younger daughter – Elspeth Brodie

This isn't the end – it's just the beginning. Now it's straight to work. Some winners only find out on Sunday – and they're meeting up in Leeds on Monday afternoon.

RUTH ABRAM,

'Jesus Christ, I'm on *Emmerdale!*'

They're to be thrown straight in at the deep end – before the crew that's come to film them getting the result leaves their house, each member of the new family has been told about a spin-off video. They're handed the 130-page script and told they'll start work on it on Thursday afternoon, filming starts on Friday, and continues over the next weekend. Naturally, they'll be expected to have learnt the script by then. They'll start filming for *Emmerdale* itself a week on Monday, the day after they're done with the location filming for the video. They'll get the first ten scripts for that, representing their first full recording block, next week, the following fifteen the week after that. The following weekend, they'll be shooting additional scenes for the video in Leeds. Then there will be another full week on *Emmerdale*. They'll probably get the following weekend off, but that will depend on press and publicity demands on them.

The *Soapstars* and *Emmerdale* people are desperate to keep the secret of who's won. The last ten are sworn to secrecy, and even have to sign something to that effect; they aren't even told on the day they find out whether they've won who else has made it. So, it's only when they do meet up at the 'safe house' outside Leeds, on Monday evening, that they know for certain who they'll be working with.

The safe house is a farmhouse, with four bedrooms. Ruth and Elspeth share a room, just like their characters Jess and Lucy do, but – at this early stage, at least – without the tension ('They're thick as thieves,' Jason says). They'll spend three days here, learning scripts. They're visited by Keith Richardson and Steve Frost, and all of them agree they are well looked after, but it's a little claustrophobic for some of them. They're not meant to leave the house, but some of them do sneak off for walks or to pop to the pub. Tuesday, Wednesday and Thursday morning are spent going through some of the basics – what's expected of them, and there's a little screen coaching (although not as much as originally planned, as Steve doesn't deem it necessary). They find out what they'll be paid, and what will be in their contracts. They're given their *Emmerdale* scripts to learn for the following week. Most skim them, but don't begin learning them yet. Jason, a real fan of the show, avidly checks the scripts to find out what's going to happen next in the series.

One visitor is Lance Milligan, *Emmerdale's* costume designer. One often-overlooked aspect of creating a new character is costuming, but many classic soap characters are almost defined by what they wear – Hilda Ogden's pinny, Bet Lynch's earrings, Mandy Dingle's leopard print.

'I'm not given a specific budget for each character, I get to divide up a pool of money how I see fit, really,' Lance reveals. 'Most of it, obviously, is dictated by the requirements of the scripts – *Emmerdale* is fond of theme nights, where people get to put on fancy dress, and there are also things like the Vets' Ball and Lady Tara's posh parties where the women get to wear ballgowns.'

There's no one source for Lance's costumes. 'For the day-to-day stuff, I buy a composite wardrobe for a new character, three or four complete changes of clothes that can be mixed and matched. That would normally cost six or seven hundred pounds a character – but that really depends: I get the Dingles' clothes from charity shops, Lady Tara has real designer gear, or very good copies.

'These are characters, not people, and the costuming has to reflect their character,' Lance explains. 'I've also got to be careful to give people a distinct "look" – for example, we've got a lot of teenagers at the moment, and it's important to distinguish them visually.' He relies on intuition for a lot of his costuming decisions. 'The scripts rarely specify what clothes people wear, but you can pick up hints from their backgrounds and the sort of job they do. You also have to think about the sort of scenes they play. With the new family, for example, we're going to be seeing them all together a lot at home at night and at breakfast, so they've all got to have nightwear.'

Lance thinks that *Emmerdale*'s new family are fairly well defined. 'Maggie's sensible, practical and organized. Her clothes reflect that. They aren't very adventurous, but Maggie knows she suits blue, from a powder blue through to a royal blue, and a lot of her clothes are that colour.

'Phil is smart, controlled, and a little old-fashioned, but he's got a bit of money. His clothes reflect that, they are conservative, but good quality.

'The script of the video specifies that Jess wears Dolce and Gabbana. That fits in with her being slightly older than her years and being a bit spoilt.' Although this taste for D and G is reflected in Jess's wardrobe, however, not much of it is genuine. Lance also has practical considerations to weigh up when choosing outfits for the actors. 'I had to bear in mind what Ruth was doing in the video – a lot of running, and in crowds. That meant flat shoes and jeans. Because there were going to be high angles, and we want her to stand out from the crowd, I've given her a red leather coat.

'Lucy is younger, and her upbringing was less prosperous. Her mother's influence is obvious – her stuff is more practical, less flashy than Jess's. She's younger, less confident. I suspect living with Jess is going to rub off on her, and we'll start to see that influencing her wardrobe.' Lance has also got together a Hotten Comp school uniform for Lucy, as she is in the fifth form.

'Craig is also Maggie's child, and her influence has rubbed off on him, too, but he's a little older, so he's got more of an individual look,' Lance says. 'Again, though, there's something practical about the clothes – jeans and cord jackets. Craig's also distinct from the other male characters around that age – Scott Windsor, for example, goes for sharp suits.'

Although Lance was supplied with character outlines, measurements and head shots, he was not able to have access to the actors themselves until relatively late in the day. This is in marked contrast to the way he would usually work on *Emmerdale*. 'I went out to the safe house with some of the wardrobe, but if something didn't work, I'd have to go all the way back to the studio for something else. It eats into your time, and obviously there are other demands on it. Sometimes with new actors, we'd go clothes shopping together in Leeds – in this case they didn't want them to be seen in public before the result was known. But I was able to speak to all the actors, talk things through, and I'm pleased with the results.'

Lance feels that the demands of outfitting the cast of a modern soap such as *Emmerdale* are more exacting than those for an historical piece, although he doesn't always feel this is acknowledged…. 'I think it's a shame the BAFTAs always go to period pieces – they've got a huge budget and it's relatively easy to see the effort that's gone into the costumes. Contemporary drama's a lot more difficult – one pet hate of mine is seeing people walk into a room who look like they've just walked out of the changing cubicle in a shop. The first thing I do with new clothes is put them in the laundry two or three times to take that sheen off, get the hanger lines out of them, make them look like clothes, not costumes. But I take it as a great compliment when I tell someone what I do and they say, "Oh, I thought the actors just turned up in their own clothes."'

blackpool

Friday 28 September to Sunday 30 September
After a few days, there's a little bit of cabin fever setting in, and the new family are all keen to start filming.

The press haven't found them, but they have come to the attention of the police. Neighbours have seen anonymous vans arriving at the farmhouse, they've seen the drawn curtains, they've seen the house taking delivery of mysterious silver boxes (the *Soapstars* equipment cases and other supplies) and have got suspicious. The police arrive, in some numbers, to make sure the house isn't being used by a terrorist cell. Fortunately, it isn't too difficult to convince them that the new family in *Emmerdale* aren't followers of Osama bin Laden.

On Thursday afternoon, the family are whisked away to Blackpool for their first acid test, the filming of the spin-off video, due out on 7 November, the day they make their first appearance on *Emmerdale*. It's a thirty-five-minute one-off story, written by *Emmerdale* writer Karin Young, and covers the day before the family decide to move to Emmerdale; we see them drive off towards their new home at the end.

It's not going to ease the new actors in to their roles, that's for sure. For the video, just about every scene has at least one member of the family in it. In most scripts, they'd be in a handful of scenes. Even in Episode 3042, their first, designed to bring them into the series with a bang, they're only in eight scenes out of the twenty-four.

On Friday, filming starts in Pontins, with nine scenes scheduled for the day. All the new family are needed – Dee and Mark are required on set at eight in the morning, which means Dee's picked up at six-thirty, Mark at seven, to go into make-up. Elspeth and Jason get a bit more of a lie-in – they're on set at nine. Ruth isn't required on location most of the day – she's not required until a quarter to five. But she goes off to plan the big chase scene she'll start filming that night, which will take most of the next day to complete. The new family have quickly got used to the call sheet – a document that's almost as long as the script and that details exactly where everyone should be, when they should be there, how they get there, and what they'll be doing once in place. To prevent leaks, the names of the actors who make up the new family aren't on the call sheet, which is a little self-defeating, but this doesn't confuse anyone for long. Friday's filming goes smoothly.

Tim Fee, as well as being line producer, is the producer of this video: 'The crew we're using on the video are all *Emmerdale* people, extending themselves once again. At the moment, for a few weeks, we're "triple stranding" on the show – making fifteen episodes a fortnight instead of "only" ten, which we need to do from time to time to keep ahead of ourselves. So, it's our busiest time of year, but we can still stretch ourselves to do this.

'This is the sixth video in eight years,' Tim explains, 'and this year we've also done hour-long episodes; we've done *This Morning* and a show for Irish TV, *The Kelly Show*, live from our studio floor. There wouldn't be any point doing it if the quality suffered, so we make sure the quality doesn't suffer. But it's always good to do something different, to meet the challenge, and the videos always do extremely well.

'To make even more work for ourselves, we always end up with a chase scene in the videos – gondolas in the Venice one, through the cane fields in "Dingles Down Under". This year it's a chase down the front in Blackpool, with trams, a clown and a Grumbleweed, shot on a busy Saturday afternoon, with crowds and traffic all around us.' Tim's enjoyed the location this time around, though: 'It's been fun working on the front and pier at Blackpool, and at Pontins. Last night, we had some great fun at the Pleasure Beach, and we were just finishing off as the lights started coming on.

'This year, of course,' he acknowledges, 'we faced the great unknown – the new family. It's a refreshing change, thinking about it – we're away from Emmerdale with a completely new set of actors. But it wouldn't matter what we planned, the end result depends on the talent of the actors. And no one at *Emmerdale* apart from Steve knew the result, or was involved, so none of us knew what we were getting until a few days ago.' Having seen the *Soapstars* winners going through their paces, however, Tim pronounces himself very satisfied: 'They've sent us five good actors, they've really been terrific. I've been phoning

TIM FEE, *Emmerdale's* line producer

'The test in the long run will be their stamina and how receptive they are. They're signing autographs already, they've got people coming up to them who recognize them, and that's great at first, but it won't seem like fun when they're tired and it still doesn't stop.'

people, telling them not to worry, now I've seen them in action, and I know other people on the crew have, too.'

Tim makes a point about another aspect of life as a TV actor: 'Stepping into that Green Room for the first time isn't going to be easy,' he notes. 'They'll have forty pairs of eyes staring at them. Now, they're already a group, they've been through a lot together, they're all in the same boat – they're all in the same house, at the moment. That could help them. But from what I've seen this weekend, the existing cast are going to see these people are up to the job. When that happens, they'll be welcomed in. Our commitment has always been to our cast, and to the programme, and the new family are part of that cast now and they won't let the side down.'

Ruth has the most to do on Saturday, as almost every scene is part of a chase down the sea front at the beginning of the video. The chase is filmed in segments – the first just outside an amusement arcade, the second a little further up the road, a third along the sea front, a fourth at the tram at one end of the North Pier, and the finale at the end of the North Pier. Each one needs to be shot more than once, to catch the action from a different angle. In addition, as the chase is in a public place, not the controlled environment of the studio or the village set, there are plenty of things that can go wrong – planes overhead, police sirens, members of the public shouting or getting into shot. Plenty of hen parties stagger by. One particularly lengthy scene takes about eight or nine takes – and also takes its toll on Ruth, who has to run in every one of them.

A crowd's gathered. This was anticipated, of course – police and traffic wardens are on hand to make sure nothing gets out of hand. Most people are fascinated by the proceedings, at least at first. Most drift away after two or three takes of the same scene. Not everyone knows what's going on – one woman seems to think director Tim Dowd is Clint Eastwood. A lot of people assume it's *Coronation Street* at first. A couple of the more observant spot the Tate Haulage lorries (in reality, cunningly disguised production vehicles), and put two and two together.

A few people have even recognized the Soapstars:

- 'It's the new family for *Emmerdale*.'

- 'Who's the daddy? Heh heh. Who's the daddy?'

- 'Like *Popstars*, only they're getting a new family.'

- 'But they haven't picked them yet. That's tonight, so why are they here now?'

- 'She's definitely one of them. I don't recognize him.'

- 'That's the girl in the Harry Potter T-shirt who cries and hits people.'

- 'That's not a Harry Potter T-shirt.'

- 'I'm sure that's Lisa Dingle. Do I mean Lisa Dingle?'

- 'Is the little Indian girl there? She's really horny.'

– 'And the music's that Fatboy Slim track.'

– 'I'm glad he won, I didn't like the other one. Too full of himself.'

Between takes, the new family circulate when they get a chance. Jason and Elspeth are given Blackpool souvenirs by a couple of old women. Ruth signs autographs. Elspeth signs a postcard for someone's granddaughter.

It's the last scene of the day that's worrying Ruth the most. She's got to stand at the end of the pier, and threaten to jump. It will involve standing on a small platform forty feet above the sea. Ruth came down to the site yesterday, and is determined to do it, but there is a stuntwoman for some of the more dangerous parts. 'Let's try to get this in one take,' Ruth laughs, a little nervously. In the event, she's up there for the best part of an hour, but does almost everything herself, tethered in place in a harness that's concealed under her costume. Director Tim Dowd is impressed, and so's Tim Fee.

Elspeth and Jason haven't much to do – there are a couple of scenes involving a broken-down car on the sea front, and they've each got a couple of lines in the scene at the end of the pier. But the weather's far better than you'd expect at the end of September. There's not a cloud in the sky, so they're happy to sit on the sea front and wait to be called.

All five members of the new family are happy to be here. They don't have any regrets, at least not yet. They're looking forward to tonight, when the result is broadcast, so they can finally tell people beyond their immediate family where they've been for the last week. Jason wants to go onto the Emmerdale set. They've still not been to the Emmerdale studio, and have only visited the village the once, during the finals, before they knew the results. They won't have long to wait: they've got a scene in the Woolpack on Monday afternoon (although Jason only has one line). Dee thinks she's died and gone to heaven – she's enjoying everything, from the chance to play a meaty part to having someone else do her make-up. Elspeth's a little bored today, because she's not got much to do. She's keen to work.

For the second day running, all the scenes are completed to schedule. Tim Fee and video director Tim Dowd are happy with the day's work. They retire for an evening meal – and they've arranged a TV to be there, to watch the broadcast of the announcement.

When the announcement is made, the press makes a great deal of these 'unknowns' coming in to *Emmerdale*. The papers report that only Mark Jardine has any acting experience. Actually, that isn't the case – all five have been paid for some acting work, all five have formal acting training, and some television experience. Between them, the five have been acting for something like sixty or seventy years. It is, of course, a better story to say that the people have come from nowhere to win, but it's not entirely accurate....

the new family, in their own words

MARK JARDINE
'I finished a degree in Sociology at Leeds University, and I went to the States, teaching fencing and soccer at a summer camp, believe it or not. I'd learned fencing at school, my claim to fame until now was that I fenced for Leicestershire, once, when I was thirteen. I got back from

America and my mum had arranged an interview to be a sociologist, and I got that. I hadn't kept in touch with anyone from school, and hardly anyone from university, so I joined a drama group to meet people and get my social life going again. I saw an advert in the *Leicester Mercury* for the Lansdowne Drama Workshop.... I joined that, right in the middle of a production, so it was too late to get a part, but I ended up working on the lighting.

'I was really enjoying myself, making friends. The next production was *The Man From Galilee*, which was one of those religious rock shows that were everywhere in the late seventies, early eighties. That was in 1982. I played Pontius Pilate. I was already in a couple of theatre groups by then, like the Little Theatre of Leicester, which Richard Attenborough is a patron of. I did music hall stuff, too.

'My day job was on the Manpower Services Commission, as a sports and recreation officer. I was doing proper drama training now, at a place called East 15, who had three schools around the country. It was a nice atmosphere, the training was heavily into "the method", the Stanislavsky approach. I applied for a postgrad course, but it had to be for three years, and I could barely afford one, but you got a scholarship if you did odd jobs for them. So I quit my job, and became a full-time member of the entertainment industry, doing all sorts of things. Since then, I've only worked as a performer, I've not had a "normal job".

'I was a Blue Coat, just like my character Phil was – I was in Scarborough, not Blackpool. And Phil hopefully lasted more than six weeks. I got sacked for calling bingo numbers too slowly. That was in the summer of 1986. I was earning my Equity Card – which was a lot harder in those days, you had to have had a certain number of contracts. I did what most people did, and took the variety route. I did a comedy routine – that was the real height of alternative comedy, and that's what I did – I was a singer, a cabaret artist. I was a dancer – I'm not a brilliant dancer, but there wasn't much competition on the Leicester cabaret scene, so I did OK. I was also doing some extra work on television – I was a knight in *Doctor Who*, I did other things like that.

'I was starting to get some substantial work by then. I was in *Grease: The Musical*, a production with Tamzin Outhwaite, who's in *EastEnders* now, and Joanne Farrell who's in the new *Crossroads*. I did *Blood Brothers* in Ireland, I was in *Patsy Cline the Musical*, which somehow managed to get into the West End for a ten-week run. I moved to London in 1994, when an ex-girlfriend told me about a place. I was doing everything by then – I was a Singing Telegram (not a strippergram – I sang Sinatra songs), I was a Country and Western DJ in Essex. I was a shopping centre promoter, someone who presents those displays. I even did that in Seattle, not that you could tell, because every shopping centre looks the same.

'I didn't have a game plan – my aim was to keep going, not to close off any avenues, while paying the bills. But it wasn't always possible to get in to auditions. Once you've done musicals, say, everyone in the world, from your agent onwards, seems to think you can *only* do that, that you actively can't do anything else. I wanted to be on TV or in film, but wasn't sure how to do it. I'd been brought up on telly and film and holiday camp humour, and I wanted to do that, but I wasn't getting very far. At the Millennium I'd just hit forty, and I moved back to Leicester, and I think my agent thought that meant I was on the verge of giving up.

WHAT THE PAPERS SAY

The first day the new family go to the *Emmerdale* studio for filming, the *Daily Star* front page news is that the *Emmerdale* cast will 'Make the Soapstars' Life Hell'. It's an old story, resurrecting quotes from April and May, suggesting there will be imminent strike action, suggesting that Lisa Riley is boycotting the programme in disgust (which ignores the fact she was in *Soapstars* itself, giving a cheerful pep talk to the semi-finalists), rounded off with the – bizarre – claim that the established actors have told producers they won't be in scenes with the new family. So, should we believe what we read in the papers?

Mark Jardine laughs. 'I love the idea that actors have the power to decide what lines they'll do. It just doesn't work like that. When people watch *Emmerdale*, they'll notice that there are indeed established cast members in our scenes.' Jason admits, 'I was really nervous about stepping into the Green Room and seeing the rest of the cast. But straight away, Amy [Nuttall, who plays Chloe] came over, and we had a coffee and a chat.' Elspeth echoes that. 'Everyone in the cast was really upset about that *Daily Star* thing. They made a point of coming up to us and saying that the story was all made up. And it was just complete bullsh–... nonsense. Every single word of it. The cast didn't have any preconceptions about us.' 'I think the story actually helped,' Ruth says. 'It gave the cast a reason to come up to us and break the ice. First over was Shirley Stelfox [Edna], who told me not to worry about it, it was all made up.' 'You know Equity issued a statement about that, retracting their comments that were quoted?' Jason asks. 'It was all rubbish. Everyone's been great.'

Elspeth's happy. 'Everyone's been so nice – Ruth and I've been out for the evening with Mark and Karl [Marc Reynolds and Robert Sugden], but everyone else has been warm with us, too. Andi Peters told me the other day – hang on, I can't believe I just said that – anyway, he said that you shouldn't believe the bad stuff, but you shouldn't believe the good stuff either. I think we've learned that already.'

I was still working – as a solo singer, doing murder mystery events – but I wasn't applying for much.

'Then *Soapstars* came along, and that really was a golden opportunity. It meant I could leapfrog so much. I didn't have to send out a thousand CVs, or get to know casting directors, or whatever it is that usually works. But I was a bit nervous – I couldn't think of anything to do for the fifteen seconds, I really didn't want to look stupid, and I was late turning up on the day at Sheffield, so they turned me away. But when they announced that adult audition, I realized I really should be there.

'What did I think of the judges? Well, now I'm so incredibly grateful. They've changed my life, and I've got them to thank. At the time, I didn't feel comfortable chatting with them. I realized they had to like you, and I know the judges had their favourites. But you never knew what they were looking for – you look at any of the last three dads – it's pretty obvious they weren't going for just one quality, or one "look" – we were all so different. I always felt I fitted the brief better, I looked more like a dad, I'm old enough to have teenage kids, although I don't have any. But you could never be sure. With *Soapstars*, a lot of the scenes weren't shown – we all understood the show wanted to be entertaining, and that they wanted to maintain an element of surprise, so they showed everyone making mistakes, everyone doing OK in other places. It wasn't always so balanced on the day.

'On set, now, the pressure isn't as intense as that – you don't get many takes, but you do get a rehearsal, you do get to talk it through and block it out. They can edit a couple of takes together, using the best bits.

'The nearest thing I've done to *Emmerdale* before was *Robin Hood*, for American TV, filmed in Lithuania. I was there for four weeks, playing a character who was in a fair few episodes – barely an extra in some of them, but a credited "guest star" in one of them. One episode every eight days, and that was a day-to-day television job. A nice one.

'I always sneered a little at the people who stay on a soap forever, but now I'm here, I can really see why they'd want to. It's such a good atmosphere, it's almost a regular Monday to Friday job, but at the same time, there's such a sense of energy, there's a chance to grow and learn. It's early days yet, but I'd love to stay here as long as possible. But after *Emmerdale*... I still don't have a career ladder or anything like that, but it would be nice to stay in TV, perhaps move on to film.'

DEE WHITEHEAD

'My first acting role? I was about thirteen or fourteen, and I played Titania in *A Midsummer's Night's Dream*. What an incredible role, I just loved that. I loved drama classes, the drama teacher encouraged me, and I played all sorts of things after that, but no one ever said, "Why don't you think about becoming an actress?" It wasn't that sort of school. I was very rebellious at school. I always loved talking to people, but I was always told at school I was "too much", I was slapped down. Thinking about it now – who I am now – I've always been that way, but I've always allowed other people to influence me. So I've always worried about being "too much".

'I went into hairdressing very young, at thirteen. I always looked older. I got into nightclubs when I was thirteen. When I was fourteen I met Paul. Outside a chip shop! He had a fabulous scooter, he'd got all these mirrors on it. He was going out with a friend of mine, Elaine, and he offered her a lift. And I stood there saying "What about me?", and he said he'd come back for me. He ended up having a massive row with my friend, and they split up. But two weeks later we started going out. I felt guilty, because Elaine was my best friend, and she'd told me so much about Paul. In the end, Elaine wasn't bothered.

'I can't remember ever having ambitions. I took each day as it came. I enjoyed the creativity of hairdressing, and meeting people. I was good at what I did. When I went self-employed, I got hundreds of clients. I wasn't acting, but I was in my brother-in-law's band, off and on, so I was busy. I got engaged to Paul on my eighteenth birthday. I got married at twenty, had the boys. Then it was the usual – sleepless nights, no money. The pressures built up, there was no time for acting or anything like that. I decided to leave my job when I got married, and on the eve of our wedding, Paul got sacked. He was a chef, and he'd booked the honeymoon as holiday, then they realized they needed him in the run-up to Christmas, and he refused to cancel the holiday, so they sacked him.

'Then, when I was twenty-six, I was on a school trip with my youngest son, who was about five. His teacher asked me "What's your dream?" I said I wanted to be an actress. The answer surprised me. It was always in the background, but so many other things had got in the way, I hadn't realized before then. I had always felt like I was showing off, I ought to hold it in check. My son's teacher suggested I joined a small theatre group where she was a member. So I went. It was like I'd come home. Nothing could keep me off the stage after that. Because I could sing and dance and smile, I always ended up in the chorus line. I used to go up for the leads, but I never got them. I was furious! That went on for years. Twelve or thirteen years! I loved it, though; we put on all sorts of productions, every couple of months. I loved the people.

'Although I was enjoying it, I was frustrated. I was always trying to be the person who everyone else wanted me to be. I didn't know who I was, I had no solidity in myself. That sometimes meant sacrificing myself. Paul was a rock, he really supported me. I was a free spirit, but I always wanted somewhere to land. But Paul and my friends, they provided that.

'As an actor, I enjoyed getting into other people's shoes. I loved the characters I was playing. But personally I felt unsure of myself. I was up and down weight-wise, I was all over the place. When I was performing on stage, though, I was a different person. I became alive up there.

'My ambition then was to be the lead in amateur dramatics. I didn't think I could go professional. All the directors I was going in front of never let me go any further. I was about to give up, then one woman, Gina Reeves, at Co-operative Arts Theatre, she saw something in me. She was setting up her own group, the Takeaway Theatre so I joined that. The first thing we did was *Teachers*, by John Godber, which I loved. I played eleven characters in that! Then she offered me *Shirley Valentine*. I was thirty-five. It's a one-woman show, and I really wasn't sure. I read the script, I loved it, but I didn't think I could do it. Then we were out with some friends, and one of them said, "You can't do it, you'd never do it", and he burst out laughing. I was on the verge of saying no, but funnily enough that comment somehow spurred me on. It was a two-week run, and I loved it, saying wonderful words that meant a lot to people. I thought I could do anything.

Then I heard about a diploma course at the local college that was part-time, so I could carry on working. There was a RADA tutor there, Geoff Bullen, who told me I had something, and I should work at it. I studied there for two years.

'I was doing twelve-hour days hairdressing, then at college most nights. I hardly ever went home. I was starting to think about becoming a professional actress. I'd got some paying work, nothing worth talking about. Gina encouraged me, and a woman called Amanda Whittington wrote a play that she wanted me to be in, they both thought I had something. But I still didn't know if I was good enough.

'I had to finish college about three years ago – I was feeling ill, I was working solidly. I snapped. I didn't do anything. I gave up the hairdressing, after nearly thirty years. I didn't cook, clean. I ate too much. I sometimes spent days at a time in my dressing gown. I was so exhausted. I was on the verge of success, but it felt like I was being "too much" again, all those childhood fears came back. It scared the hell out of me. I didn't want to be me. I became unrecognizable – I dyed my hair bright red. I got brown contact lenses.... I felt like I'd gone mad. I was ashamed that I couldn't cope. It was like playing a part. I wanted to be anyone but me. I was really confused about everything....

'I'd always had a problem with my weight. It started when I was about eight. Honestly. I was a little porker, I didn't grow out my "puppy fat" until I was thirteen. I accepted it, but as I got older, it was binge, diet, binge, diet – up two stone, down two stone. I was never anorexic or bulimic, or anything like that, but it's been like that all through my life. And time and again, I'd get the weight down, I'd start getting some attention for my acting... and I'd start eating. I'd always exercised, walked, aerobics – I stopped that. I was more than four stone overweight. Paul accepted that was how I needed to be. I was so lucky – he went through a lot, but he knew it was something I needed to work through. Paul's got his own business, and that started to suffer. He was petrified about me.

'But gradually I started to get some control. I went to someone who was recommended to me. She was a herbalist, I didn't know who else to turn to. Little things started to happen, Paul could see I was getting better. We went through therapy, realized that all the little things had snowballed. It was hellish at the time, but we got everything out into the open, learned that the most important thing was to be real with each other, with everybody. And we did soul-searching like that for three months. I started reading self-help books, and three years ago I started doing yoga. I realized I was the only person in control of my life.

'It's crazy that I wanted to be an actress, I suppose. Wanting to perform, wanting to be on stage, showing off, but also trying to draw into myself. I wanted people to know what I was like on the inside... but my job as an actress is all about appearance and external things – to be someone else. But I wanted to try, I didn't want any "what ifs" in my life. Now I know you can do anything if you put your mind to it. I went on a self-help weekend recently: you examine your "self-limiting beliefs", then you smash them. For me it was my fear of success. I ate to limit my success. I'd make myself less able to do what I really wanted to do. It was like I was putting padding around myself, to protect myself. Once I'd realized that, my weight started plummeting. Suddenly doors kept opening, I could see all these opportunities. I have this urge to perform, to be an actress, that's pushed at me all my life, but other people have tried to damp it down, and I have too. Everyone except Paul has. Paul's always been so supportive.

'It's taken me years to pull myself out of that completely, I only managed to get all the way out a couple of months before the *Soapstars* audition came along.

'I'm happy with my body, for the first time. If I carry on with my yoga, it's the way forwards, and now I *want* to eat healthily.

'I started thinking about my ambitions again. I decided my ambition is to play Mrs Johnstone in *Blood Brothers*, the Willy Russell musical, in the West End. I've got an agent, but they've told me there's no way I can do that unless I'm a "name". Barbara Dickson and Petula Clarke have played it there. So I've got to become a "name".

'Two weeks later it was the first *Soapstars* audition, and I had such a brilliant feeling about it. My worries had gone.

'I wasn't that worried about *Soapstars*. I would have been disappointed if I hadn't got it, but I felt it was my time, even if I hadn't got it, it would lead somewhere else. I just felt I should enjoy it, let be whatever would be.'

JASON HAIN

'I did an action plan, and this year I was going to get a panto (which I did – I've had to turn it down, now, of course), then by April next year, I was aiming for a couple of episodes of *Take the High Road*. This time next year, I'd have reached an episode of *Taggart* or *Rebus*. So I'm ahead of myself for the moment.

'It's early days; I'm really enjoying myself. I suppose I

see myself being here for at least a few years, if they'll have me. If they give me the boot after three months, at least I've been here, I've got the experience, people have seen me and what I can do.

'The thing that surprised me most was that we get the whole script, not just the scenes we're in. They dumped a pile of scripts on me, it was about a foot high, and I thought those were just my bits, and I'd have to learn it all. At the same time, when you're in a scene and you've only got one line, it's difficult to keep your concentration. It's good, though, you get to learn by example. I'm just watching and learning this week. The worst thing is having to shave every single day – I'd usually not have to, but here I do, to make me look younger and for continuity.

'I enjoy doing my job: getting a scene done in as few takes as possible. I've just been doing a couple of two-hander scenes with Mark – just us two, and we just did them. Straight in and out – one take, or one take with a small pick-up at the end, because a boom mike got into shot or a light went. And the director's delighted, and doesn't need to go again, so you know you're doing your job. With the scenes with the whole family, or with loads of characters, it's harder to keep your focus, it's all mechanical – you've got two, three cameras, booms, lights, you've got to be so careful where you stand. It's so much planning, and so much to go wrong.

'I've got some really fantastic stories coming up, though. It's really bad, because I can't tell my mum or my friends what they are. They all want to know what's coming up in the show. I've always watched all the soaps. I even watched *Eldorado*. Bill Lyons wrote for that – I really enjoyed it. I think I was the only one. I love *Emmerdale* – I remember Dolly and Matt and Annie Sugden in her pinny.

It's difficult to believe that I'm in it now, that there are people out there who'll reminisce about me one day. They showed us round the village during the finals, and I really wouldn't have minded if I'd been dropped that day – I got to go round Emmerdale, and you usually aren't allowed unless you're on the show. The sets are great. They seem a bit small at first, but they're really clever – the walls and things move around to let the cameras and microphones in. And they sell Irn Bru in Viv's shop – 35p a can, which is cheap, but if you look at the sell-by dates, they're best before last December.

'I graduated top of my year from the Liverpool School of Performing Arts. Brian was quick to mention that on the *Big Breakfast*, but I never hid it. Some of my friends on that course have got contracts in the West End, but I think I qualify as the first big break. I did pick cabbages over the summer, and back then I thought it was good money – I'm the only one of the five with any money at the moment, because we've not been paid yet. All that "cabbage picker" stuff was good PR. *Soapstars* concentrated on it, which is fair enough, they were making a programme. It made me the People's Champion! People remember me – they've come up to me in the street and gone, "Hey, you're that guy with the cabbage on *Soapstars*."... the people who watched it remember Johnny Kinch, and Erin, and me I suppose. Mr Cabbage. In the end, I've got the job, so now it's up to me to prove I can act. Lorraine Kelly likes me, she said so this week. And their soap woman liked me, although she thought it was a bit of a cheat because I'd been to drama school.

'I've been recognized on the street a bit. Elspeth hasn't, but I've got my eyebrows, my distinguishing feature.

They've made me pluck them, you know. Twice.

'I reckon all of the last ten, probably all of the last fifteen finalists are going on to do well. It was such a good opportunity.

'The first week's gone really quick. They're long hours, and there's a lot of hanging around waiting for your scene, but it doesn't seem like a week, not at all. I'm doing what I've always wanted to do, and it doesn't really feel like working.

'I've kept in touch with my friends and family. My dad's on the phone all the time. The best thing about *Soapstars* is that I didn't have to tell anyone I'd got the part, they did all that for me. On Monday morning, after the result had been announced, I'd got fifty cards at home, everyone I've ever known has got in touch in the last week, I think. I've had a hundred text messages a day. It's a hell of a job replying to them all. You get cramp.

'The downside? Well, my gran died last week. The funeral was on Friday, and that was the day we were filming the video, so I couldn't go. And it was silly – my parents couldn't say where I was, because it was still a secret then. I told my family, and I had to tell my boss. I guess the other cabbage pickers have twigged why I wasn't at work. But I got to say goodbye to Gran before that, and she knew I'd won.

'I got Brownie points because I watch the show, so I know all the characters' names, and I know most of the actors' names already, too. The other *Soapstars* people have been asking me who everyone is. I don't think Dee knew anyone. They gave us all these sets of publicity postcards with a picture and the names on them, to help out, another thing to learn, but I didn't need it. Paula Tilbrook [Betty] didn't

NEARLY SOAPSTARS

What do the runners-up think about the people who pipped them to the post? Now it's all over, there's a chance to dig the dirt. But you won't hear a word said against Dee. 'Dee's lovely!' Erin gushes, without hesitating. 'We all love Dee,' the others agree enthusiastically. 'I want to set up the Dee Whitehead Fan Club,' Becky says. The unanimous view is that Dee is a genuinely nice person. All five runners-up have spoken to her since they've found out the results.

They all agree Jason had a good sense of humour, and was a strong actor. A couple of the runners-up are a little more guarded about Ruth, whom they think spent more time talking to the panel than to the other hopefuls. 'She acted like she knew she'd got it from really early on,' Becky suggests. However, they all like Mark – 'He's a nice bloke', according to Brian. Becky feels that he was, 'A little odd, a bit trainspotter-ish. Nice, though.' Jo-Ann and Erin both liked him.

Becky shared a room with Elspeth at the finals, and pays a warm tribute to her: 'She was so bright and bubbly, and so intelligent – I always thought I could learn lines fast, but she was so much faster. She's really down to earth, too'. Jo-Ann and Becky also reckon Elspeth was a deserving winner – 'She was the strongest actor out of the ten girls', Jo-Ann says.

So, no hard feelings, then? 'We were all at Planet Hollywood last night,' Craig says, 'and these girls came up to us and said they'd picked the wrong ones, and they'd gone for the "uglier option". I think we'd all agree with that!'

believe me, and she tested me, but she's happy now because she couldn't catch me out. But, of course, I don't know any of the behind-the-scenes people, and there are just as many of those. So I keep going back to the video – you think, "OK, he's doing what Tim Dowd did, so he's the director, and the director is Ollie, so he must be Ollie." It doesn't help that they're making three blocks at once at the moment, so there are three whole crews to learn the names of.

'The dog's adorable, a really good stress reliever. But at the moment, she's got a bit of a mind of her own, she doesn't know she's on telly.

'I'm glad I'm getting some scenes away from the rest of the family. It's so easy to get irritated with each other – we're sharing a house, we're dead busy, up really early, then at weekends it's the video. So you spend all day together. Everyone's lovely, and we all know what we've been through, so we're supportive. But you need a break.'

RUTH ABRAM

'I've been acting since I was about seven – my first professional job was in *Mother Goose*, when I was twelve. Dancing was my thing, though. I went to the Northern Ballet School for a year. Then I started a joint drama/dance degree at the University of Central Lancashire, and drama was more work, but I found it more satisfying. I was just finishing off the course when the *Soapstars* audition came up.

'I've done quite a bit of stage work – dance shows, mostly, but I was a witch in *The Witches* in Birmingham. I've been an extra on television – walk-on parts on *Brookside* and *Hollyoaks*. A couple of weeks ago, I was an extra on *Ted and Alice*, a new Stephen Tompkinson series.

'I've always wanted to be in contemporary drama, like a soap. I watch all the soaps, and I did watch *Emmerdale* before all this. The last week, though, it's weird, there's no time to watch them any more.

'I got through the fifteen seconds stage in eight

seconds? Excellent. I knew that at that point they were just seeing how we looked and sounded and moved about. I didn't spend any time preparing for it. I took a plastic bag on stage, and it had my lunch in, and I just told them that, and I got through. I was at the first audition – 8 June, and I was in the first group. So I've been living with this *Soapstars* thing for so long now. I was lucky, though – I started queuing at half-seven and they saw me by half-nine.

'I did seem to be crying all the time on *Soapstars*, but that was good: it meant I got a sympathy vote. I didn't really cry that much, and definitely not when I was working. If you were there, you'd know it really was tense, there was so much waiting to hear if you were through. Everyone got to know each other really well – so many of us have stayed in touch, it's incredible – so we were losing good friends at every stage. What set me off at the semis was Katie Heppel getting rejected. I'd kept it all together until then, but she was crying, so I started crying. But they didn't just show me crying, there was me slapping Debra, and you saw me acting in a lot of scenes, so I hope I just came across as a normal person.

'Who did I think would win? I really didn't know, but I knew Elspeth would do well. Gemma Baker, too, she was good. I saw them as the competition. But there wasn't an inch of me that thought I'd got it. I know what Becky's said, but I just don't recognize the description – it was the same for everyone, no one mingled with everyone, I don't think I was any more pally with the panel than anyone else. I certainly wasn't snubbing anyone, I just don't know where she got that from, or why she felt the need to say it. I suppose that's my first negative publicity. It goes with the job. I accept that, I just hope no one drags my family into any of it. It's nothing to do with them.

'The video's good for Jess, she's got a lot to do. A lot of running! I was running all day for two days solid, then they hung me off the pier. My legs are really stiff. I got a suntan in Blackpool – I saw this mark on my chest, I thought it was make-up, but it was a tanline. But it's fantastic. It's a shame, really, we've gone straight from being told to starting work, we've not had time for it to sink in. It's good, though. Really good.

'The first week on the job has been incredible. Knackering, but really good fun. I've just done a scene that took an hour and a half, but you lose all track of time. You think it's about eleven in the morning, then it goes dark.

'What's surprised me most is how friendly everyone has been. Absolutely everyone – the producers, the actors, the crew, the canteen ladies. People always go on about family atmospheres, and one big happy team, but it's so true here. It's because everyone's so proud of what they're doing. They're even nice to the extras. I've been an extra in other things, and you usually get treated like dirt.

'I think I've got a brilliant character. I'm really looking forward to seeing where Jess goes, the trouble she gets into. I'm so happy to be here. I was doing a scene this afternoon, and halfway through it, my mind went "reality check ... I'm standing in Emmerdale. Jesus Christ, I'm in *Emmerdale*!"'

ELSPETH BRODIE

'I've been acting for ten years, and I'm only nineteen!

'Recently, I've done corporate videos and radio plays, but I was on an advert for Atlantic Telecom, and also appeared in brochures and leaflets and things for that. I did an HNC in drama, and I was just about to start a drama degree in Edinburgh. I started it at the beginning of September, the week after the finals, because I had no idea if I was going to get this or not. So I spent three weeks on the course, and to be honest I thought I was only being considered for Jess, and I was pretty sure Ruth had got it.

'I've always wanted to be an actor. I hated school, and I told my guidance teacher I wanted to be an actor, and they said don't be so ridiculous, and kept going on about fall-back plans. School wasn't any support at all. I didn't even do my Higher there, I went to an acting school. My parents really encouraged me, it's not a showbiz family – none of them even wanted to be filmed when they came round to my house to announce the result – but it's a really support-ive one. I was always the loud one.

'It's going really well, though. I'm not in every script. I think I'm only in three of the first ten. In one way that's good, because it means I've got the time to get the hang of it. On the other hand, I get paid per episode, so it would be nice to do more! I know it's not a reflection on me – these scripts were written months ago. I guess the writers didn't want to have too much of us at first, because they didn't know who we were.

'I don't think there's a problem playing the sixteen-year-old. I still am a teenage girl. Lucy's a bit of a blank canvas. She's normal, and she's young, so there's plenty of stuff she's never done which I'll get to act. There's scope for change there, she's a normal sixteen-year-old girl, and, you know, those are really the most interesting years, and the others are all past that. She's a good example of a lot of girls, I think. I'm keen on being a good role model. There are hardly any Scottish people on TV, and they're all evil, so I want to change that. Think of the soaps – there aren't that many Scottish people anyway, but there was that Callum in *Brookside*, there's Trevor from *EastEnders*. Evil. See what I mean?

'I'm not too worried about wearing a school uniform. It's not *that* long since I wore one for real. I suppose I'll get dodgy letters, but it's such a frumpy thing. It's a bit of a laugh. It's odd, though, it really helps me get into character, and I look younger when I wear it.

'My close friends seem to be quite relaxed about it. My family are really, really pleased. They had a party back home the night of the TV announcement and they phoned up to say what a great time they were having. I suppose that's the downside – I'm so far from home, and my family and my boyfriend. I'm living in a different country, and it's a bit of a culture shock. So much has happened in the last two weeks, it's difficult to keep up with the changes. I'm not really settled yet – I don't mean in the show, but we've gone from a safe house to a hotel in Blackpool to a temporary house. Next week we'll get somewhere a bit more permanent, and I'll get to unpack my suitcase.

'It's weird. I'm working from six in the morning to eight at night most days, and it doesn't bother me at all. In any other job, I'd be looking at my watch after the first hour and working out when it was time to go home. There's no way I'd have worked a fourteen-hour shift, seven days a week. But I'm enjoying this so much.

'I was recognized in Blackpool, but I've been out shopping in Leeds on my own and no one was staring or anything. I wasn't really in *Soapstars* that much, which suits me, really, so why would anyone recognize me? When Ruth and I were out in the pub the other night with Anthony and Karl, we kept being elbowed out the way by people who knew who they were, and in the end we started going, "Hey, we're famous, too, you know!" To be honest, I'm enjoying this little lull – I'm sure as soon as the first *Emmerdale* goes out people will recognize us.'

the runners-up

1 October to 5 October

It's certainly not over for those that didn't make it. The five runners-up are contacted by *The Big Breakfast*, and become the (Nearly) Family of the Week for the first week of October. It's a good consolation prize – a chance to appear on television again, show off their talents and personalities, and get a bit of sympathy. Ironically, given all the talk of the winners facing early mornings, the runners-up find themselves having to get up several hours earlier than the eventual *Soapstars* winners did for their first day on *Emmerdale* – their car picks them up from the hotel at a quarter to six.

The first day sees Erin showing off a little of the roller-skating she learned for *Starlight Express*, and Jo-Ann announcing she's available for presenting work. The show's host, Richard Bacon, appears a little disconcerted to discover that all five have already been offered work or had interest from agents after appearing on *Soapstars*. All five look relaxed and happy. They're cheered by the news that the 'Flopstars', the five *Popstars* runners-up, who formed their own band Liberty, have got to number five with their debut single, against strong opposition.

It's also the day that the *Daily Star* prints a story saying that the existing cast will give the new family hell. The runners-up are asked what they think of this, and they are pretty dismissive. When Richard Bacon mentions the 'cabbage picker', Craig in particular is keen to stress that everyone in the finals was an experienced actor, and that it 'suited *Soapstars*' to portray them as novices. Brian adds that Jason's just graduated from drama school.

With the runners-up all together in one place, there's a chance to catch them all together and see what they feel about *Soapstars* with a couple of weeks' worth of hindsight. What did they *really* think?

First of all, what about the audition process? Becky 'really enjoyed it', a sentiment all the others echo. For Erin, 'it was a great learning experience, and I was humbled to be around such great actors'. However, not everyone is so effusive. Brian's got a few reservations: 'It was good to be there, but the process began to weigh you down. My hotel room was by some roadworks, and I wasn't sleeping. But it was good experience.' For Craig it was all about personal development – 'I wanted to see how far I could go. I knew I was borderline, because of my age.'

Was it a fair test of their abilities? Jo-Ann's first to answer that one – 'I didn't feel I had emotional scripts,' she muses, 'they all seemed to be on one level.' Becky, also up for the part of Lucy, agrees – 'They were limited. Elspeth was at a huge advantage, because she was up for both parts, so she got a range of material.' Jo-Ann adds, 'Sometimes you'd be handed a script and told "Just say it", and that wasn't the best way to demonstrate your ability.' Craig also feels there were some unhelpful restrictions in the auditioning process: 'The scenes for the sons were less interesting, so there was less chance to stretch yourself.'

Did *Soapstars* give a fair representation of them? Erin laughs: 'Well, they said I was thirty-eight, and I'm thirty-seven, so they weren't that wrong.' Brian, shaking his head, counters with: 'They said I was born in Scotland, and I was born in Sydney, so that's about as wrong as you can get.' 'I don't think it hurt anyone,' Erin argues. 'Personally, I couldn't believe my luck. I wish they'd shown some of my better scenes – they only seemed to show the ones we messed up.' Jo-Ann agrees with her on that point – 'they showed that quote with Keith saying I was "affected", then cut away. But on *Soapstars Extra* they showed the whole scene, and Steve and Paul went on to say it wasn't a problem and they liked me.' Craig maintains that he was generally satisfied with the way he came across on screen: 'I was happy, especially with the showcase on the last programme. I don't think it's done anything but help me.' However, he does have one criticism to make: 'I wish they hadn't taken out every reference to my acting experience... the nearest they got was "Craig has some experience as an actor." It isn't a big deal because I'm so thankful to Tim, Paul, Yvon and Bill for the coverage, but I actually got full Equity in '95, have done several good, well-paid jobs and – most importantly – have had several near-misses for that big break. In terms of training I've probably built up more than the equivalent of a postgrad.'

Brian agrees with that sentiment – 'They were interviewing us all, all the time, but they only used one clip of me, over and over, that one about "hod carrier or Soapstar?" I'm not a bricklayer – I've done that for two months to pay the bills. But it was a better story for them to say we'd come in off the street. Look at Jason – they showed him picking cabbages, they didn't show him being handed a big cheque by Paul McCartney for graduating top of his class at the Liverpool School of Performing Arts.' And his representation has already had a bearing on at least one post-*Soapstars* audition: 'I went to a casting for an advert last week, and I had to spend the whole time telling people I was really an actor, I've been in Equity since '95, and been in at least two shows a year since then. They don't think we're actors, because we weren't shown as actors.' Becky smiles in agreement. 'Yeah, I was "Temp Becky". I didn't do anything extrovert or silly, so they didn't show me much. Which I'm happy with, I think I always looked professional. To be honest, I think they were after a bit more from me.' Becky has no gripe with the judges over their decision to pass over her, although she does feel that her concerns as an actor and those of the TV programme makers were sometimes not the same: 'When Bill came round and told me I hadn't got it, I wasn't that upset, I just had a good chat with Bill, he gave me loads of encouragement. I think the *Soapstars* people were a bit disappointed I didn't burst into tears. It was an audition, not a TV show, sometimes they seemed to forget that, but I didn't.'

Craig has another point to raise. 'Equity hasn't helped here – slagging the whole thing off without really understanding how meticulous and tough the whole process was. I've found their shortsightedness disappointing: are we all traitors to our union for going for a job – a job which will result in an Equity approved contract?' However, he's not one to dwell on things: 'For me, the positive vastly outweighs the negative – the wonderful thing about *Soapstars* is that it opens the door to those who maybe have talent but no training, no nepotistic advantages, a low-grade agent etc. – at least one of these disadvantages must have applied to every one of the final ten of us.' And he pays tribute to the judges and Tim for giving him 'the best chance I've ever had to show people I have something and thereby start my career and get to work without worrying about the rent. At the end of the day I'll have no problem saying I owe my success to a huge, gruelling open audition.'

Jo-Ann suggests, 'They wanted a cliffhanger, and so they hung it all around the "has Jo-Ann made the right decision?" thing. But the main criticism I have is that they should have shown Adrian and Ide – some people didn't get shown at all.' It was Gemma I felt sorry for,' Erin confides. 'they didn't show her at all, and she got down to the last three [Jesses].' Craig remembers there was a bit of Gemma at the end, but both Becky and Jo-Ann agree there should have been more – 'She was a better actress than Ruth.'

Craig sympathizes with Tim: 'They want the excitement of it, they wanted good TV. I took it really well, I have been here before. I've always followed that Noël Coward quote: "Your capacity for success is measured by your ability to deal with failure." You need to be able to handle rejection if you're an actor.'

So, who came out well from the show? 'Ashra was a good actress,' Becky says. Erin suggests 'Johnny Kinch was the one character who stood out.' Brian says, 'I thought Johnny did, but there was a weird reaction against him. This morning on the *Big Breakfast*, Christopher Biggins came over and said he was sorry I didn't get it, and he hoped the bald chap hadn't won.' 'He'll get work,' Jo-Ann says. Erin admits, 'I've been stopped quite a lot – someone was looking at me on the Tube and came over and said, "Don't I recognize you from the telly?" It's all very positive, everyone saying they were rooting for me.'

Have they had offers? Well, they're all on the *Big*

Breakfast this week, but aren't getting paid, although it is all expenses paid. Truth be told, they're all a little disappointed with the first couple of days – they don't think they've had much time to establish themselves as individuals, or to demonstrate their talents. They hope the last couple of shows will give them more to do.

But there are other options on the horizon. Erin, Jo-Ann and Becky have been in talks to do a shoot for a lads' mag. 'The sexy mum, posing with her two sexy daughters,' Erin laughs. 'It's every man's fantasy... apparently.' Does she want to do it? 'Oh yes – nice lighting, cover up the cellulite, who wouldn't?' Jo-Ann turned down the chance to pose for *FHM* a couple of months ago – 'They were running a feature on "sexy students" and I was spotted by someone,' she recalls. 'I didn't want to do that, but this is OK, because it could lead somewhere.' A lot of presenters have risen above the pack by doing a shoot like this. Exposure of a different kind is worrying Becky – 'I don't want to wear a bikini, because you'll see my legs.' 'She's worried about her legs,' Erin says, shaking her head in disbelief.

Craig's had a film offer, and is in discussions for a TV part that he can't talk about. He's got ambitions – 'I want to be an international British actor. Action films, if I can, but interesting parts within that. Stuff like Johnny Depp and John Cusack are doing. I don't want fame, but if I get it, I hope I can use it to make a contribution to animal welfare.' In the shorter term, he's hoping to upgrade his agent.

Brian? 'So far, there's been nothing at all, but it's early days. I'm not sure the programme's done anything but damage. They made some pretty damaging comments – they crucified me on the last but one programme. There was all that stuff about "He thinks he's got it", and no I didn't. I never thought that for a minute. I don't want fame. I want to be a successful actor.'

Jo-Ann applied for a presenting job on satellite TV a few weeks ago, only to be told they already had an Asian presenter, so they didn't need another one. But now she's been on *Soapstars* they want to see her, and seem keen. She's got a new agent too; it's early days, but things look promising. 'I don't want to rule anything out – I'm a singer, a dancer, I can act, but *Soapstars* has been a bit of a turning point,' she says. 'I love to act, and I'm a lot happier and more confident about that, now, but it would be good to establish myself as a presenter, then work from that.'

Becky's focused on acting. 'I don't want fame. I want to be successful in film and drama,' she maintains. 'I did a film, and I really enjoyed it. That's proper acting for me. On a soap, it's one character, and it's all set in one place. A film is different every day, you can get completely into a character.' If anything, her determination seems to have become stronger after her *Soapstars* experience. 'I don't want to be a temp, I want to be a full-time actor; hopefully I can start by getting parts in stuff like *Casualty*, comedies, the odd murder mystery. Jason, Elspeth and Ruth have gone straight into a job from drama school, they won't have to audition for years and years.'

Sony are re-releasing a single of Erin's. She's also getting a new agent (the same one as Jo-Ann, and Johnny Kinch). 'I phoned up, and she recognized the name and said "Oh yes, the sexy mum", so I'm getting photos and things together for that.' She's enjoyed doing the skits they've done for *The Big Breakfast*, and she's got ambitions to present – 'I'd love to do health features for *This*

Morning,' she says. 'This week, you really see how hard it is to present, though – Amanda Byram's so sharp. But I'd love to do that.' Erin wants to have some drama coaching: 'I know I got very close, and it's really given me hope, but I also know I've got a lot to learn.'

so you wanna be an actor?

In the end, despite some of the press reports, virtually all of the *Soapstars* finalists, and all of the winners and runners up, had some formal training and professional experience. But they would be the first to admit that the programme was a unique opportunity to bypass the normal system of agents and casting directors, to gain a regular part on network television.

What do you do if *you* want to be an actor?

As *Soapstars* demonstrates, thousands of people enjoy acting and they want to be famous. Many of these people think they've got a unique talent, or that their time has come. Some of them are undoubtedly right. The vast majority undoubtedly are wrong. You have to accept that, realistically, you may not have what it takes, or at the very least that you don't have what it takes *yet*. It can be hard work, and there's stiff competition.

There's no one way to become a successful actor. But anyone setting out to be an actor might want to bear in mind the following:

☐ Actors tend to be extrovert, confident, have a good speaking voice, creativity and a good memory. They should be good at observing others, and have resilience – the ability to cope with intense scrutiny and rejection.

❑ For the vast majority of actors, acting isn't glamorous or well-paid. Almost all actors, especially those starting out, supplement their income with a part-time job, or are self-employed. A lot of acting is waiting around for shots to be arranged, often in uncomfortable clothes or make-up. Actors spend a long time away from home, the working day can be extremely long and involve night filming. Most acting work is very short-term. More importantly, at any one time, four out of five actors are out of work. Only around one in twenty have acting as their only source of income. The average income from acting in the UK is less than £10,000 a year.

❑ A good preliminary step is to set up a camcorder and practise in front of it. See what you look like and sound like on television. People rarely look and sound they way they picture themselves...

❑ The best way to start can often be via amateur dramatics. Learning to sing and dance is extremely useful for stage actors. Doing modelling work means an aspiring actor can get used to the disciplines of the job, and get a good sense of how they look on camera. It can also be a good way of building up a portfolio of photographs, so people can picture you in different roles.

❑ The vast majority of working actors have formal qualifications. Gaining experience in amateur productions is more important than following any particular subjects at school, but studying English, Maths, Social Studies, Media Studies and, of course, Drama is often useful.

☐ If you've got a particular sort of acting in mind, find interviews with people who've been successful in that field, and find out how they did it. Almost all 'overnight successes' in reality involve years of plugging away, and a high degree of being in the right place at the right time.

☐ When ready, actors should circulate their CVs and a good photo to every agent, rep, theatre, casting director and TV casting department they can find.

☐ Almost every actor has an agent. Getting an agent can be a Catch-22 situation – to get an agent you need to have worked, to work you need an agent. Most actors just keep writing to different agents until someone accepts them. Agents make their money by taking a percentage of an actor's income, so it's in their interest to get work for an actor. That said, one of the most common topics of conversation when actors meet is swapping horror stories about old agents.

☐ A typical career path is a gradual building up from being an extra or 'bit' player, to small character roles, to a leading role. A lot depends on luck, and following up on contacts an actor makes at every stage. Talent is important – but so are training, versatility, perseverance and luck.

the last word...

By the end of their first week on the show, the new family have already recorded a video and are halfway to completing their first ten episodes. With *Soapstars* finished and a new family delivered safely to Leeds, Tim Miller has time to reflect on the process. Is he happy with the way *Soapstars* turned out?

'Yes. I think it's entertaining television. Some of it's also very moving.

'The punters who are featured will be happy. It's those we couldn't fit in who won't be happy.

'Not everyone, including those who progressed a long way, was featured. We just didn't have room in our half-hour shows. I feel sad that they weren't because I think everyone was hoping to benefit from the exposure. But the reality is that you need to limit your "characters" so that the viewers can identify with certain people. More than three or four characters in a programme and it gets too messy and confusing, it's harder to watch and the viewers don't care as much about the individuals.

'If I had my time again, I would keep the content more or less the same, but I would be able to get to what we wanted much quicker. We spent a lot of time in the edit re-cutting things to make the programmes work better. The basic answer was to reduce the number of characters in each programme to enable viewers to iden-tify with people more easily. It took us a while to work this out. We were trying to cram in too many people and too many stories. It all seems obvious to us now – oh the benefit of hindsight!

'It sounds very unprofessional, but the highlight was the drinking in the bar at the end of the day with the crew! When you've slept badly the night before, got up very early, worked hard under stressful conditions all day, there's something very welcome about a cool pint of lager. It was also an opportunity for everyone to have a bit of a laugh about what had been filmed that day.

'On the filming front, the best bits were when the winners were announced. You could feel the excitement and really share in people's joy. All the crew cried in Sheffield, then we got a bit hardened to it. But by the semi-finals the hankies were out again.

'It was also great to go and give people the news that they were in the final family. I did Dee and was so pleased for her. She was there with her mum, who had lost her husband during the auditions, and it was very touching hearing them both talk about it.

'The panel are certainly unforgettable. But a few of our hopefuls made an impression. Johnny "who's the daddy?" Kinch certainly made his mark. Love him, or hate him, you won't forget him. And I think the biggest star out of the family is Jason. Who could forget someone who was filmed in a blue hair-net picking cabbages?'

Would he have taken part?

'If I had been the right age, yes! Unfortunately at thirty-one, I was too old for a kid and too young for a parent. But I've done a bit of acting before. I was in an amateur production of a play, which means Bill, Yvon and Paul would have booted me out in minutes! I think I would have been a definite Day-Two loser!'

By the time the new family arrive at the Emmerdale studio to start filming, script editor Karen Grimes has edited forty scripts with them in, with another twenty storylined. The Christmas episodes are already in, and the new family will be at the heart of one of the big events that traditionally happen over Christmas and New Year in every soap. So, how easy is it to plough on without knowing who the actors are?

'It depends,' she explains. 'Most of our characters are written into scripts well before the actors are cast, so our writing team are writing for the character rather than the actor. And whoever is cast may be different from the character we pictured, and may bring something new and individual to the role. Until the roles are cast, you don't know the strengths and weaknesses of the actors, or for example their accents, so we have to be careful in terms of dialogue to write for the character, whilst also giving the actor something to work with and make their own.

'Sometimes with new characters they take a month/six weeks to hit their stride, and that's because until then the scripts aren't written with the actor in mind, and until you see the actor, you're not one hundred per cent sure who they'll work best with, what their strongest points are, etc. But in this case, we had a very strong sense of the family and where they had come from. The video script firmly establishes the characters, and there's a good family dynamic in place when they arrive in the village. It's easy for the writers to latch onto things, distinguish the new kids from the existing ones, that sort of thing.'

Out in the Holiday Village, with the family thrown together in a way that means they'll be living in a tiny chalet, squabbling amongst themselves, is there a danger they'll be out on a limb, not engaged with the rest of Emmerdale?

'Oh no,' she replies, 'they're in the Holiday Village, which means regular contact with Chris and Rodney, the owners. The Holiday Village will be a big employer, meaning several of our existing characters will end up working there. There's also rivalry between the Holiday Village and other businesses in the show. The new teenagers end up falling in with the existing ones. Phil will probably get a job in the village. The scripts we've got have them all making friends and enemies in Emmerdale. And the Holiday Village will be a big focal point for the village as Christmas approaches.'

And does Karen have a favourite character?

'From the scripts, Jess. She's got a particularly clear reason for doing what she does, and being the way she is. It's obvious a lot of the writers think she's great, too. From the video script, it's clear Maggie's also going to be a force to be reckoned with. But until you see an actor in a role, it's impossible to say. All of them have a lot of potential.'

The last word goes to Steve Frost, the producer of *Emmerdale*, who now has five new cast members to work with, and a new family that will appear in his programme. First of all, though, could we see some of those that didn't make it in other roles on *Emmerdale*?

'Possibly. Or if not, I'd be very surprised if we don't see a few of them in other programmes or adverts very soon. It's helped several good actors who just weren't quite what we wanted for *Emmerdale* to get agents and auditions.'

And what of those who did make it? Steve Frost is very pleased with the result.

'The five chosen actors are exactly what we were looking for and I think that's proof enough that it was a valid and reliable auditioning method. I'll measure how successful this process has been by the success of the story and characters that the five actors will play. I think they will do a terrific job and am very keen to see them in action.'

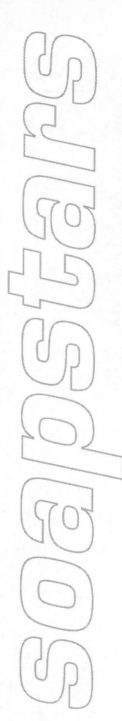

Out now – this fantastic video featuring memorable moments from the smash hit TV show, from those early nerve-wracking auditions right through to the final episode where the budding actors discover their dreams have come true. Plus a made-for-video episode featuring the dramatic events building up to the family's arrival in Emmerdale.

£14.99
Cat number: GV0402